MULTIPLE REFLECTIONS

Talks on the Yoga Vasishtha by Swami Venkatesananda

Swami Venkatesanda

MULTIPLE REFLECTIONS

Talks on the Yoga Vasishtha by Swami Venkatesananda

Compiled and Edited by
SWAMI VENKATARAMANI

CHILTERN YOGA TRUST
San Francisco
1988

Cover Design by Josh Gitomer
Typeset by Metro Typography, Santa Cruz, California
Printed by Banta Book Systems, Menasha, Wisconsin

Chiltern Yoga Foundation
1029 Hyde Street, #6
San Francisco, California 94109
USA

Contents

Acknowledgements

Grateful thanks are offered to: H.H. Sri Swami Nisreyasananda for his gracious Afterword. Swami Venkataramani for editing. Wesley Zineski and Chiltern Yoga Foundation of San Francisco for publication. Priya and Sergiu Hart of Tel Aviv for their loving assistance. The Naik family of Johannesburg for their generosity. The Pharmacy Department, Groote Schuur Hospital, Cape Town, for countless favours. Sadasiva (C.J. Hinke) for typesetting and production.

Yoga Vasistha
Prayer Before the Daily Reading

yatah sarvani bhutani pratibhanti sthitani ca yatrai 'vo 'pasamam
yanti tasmai satyatmane namah

jnata jnanam tatha jneyam drasta darsana drsyabhuh karta hetuh
kriya yasmat tasmai jnaptyatmane namah

sphuranti sikara yasmad anandasya 'mbare 'vanau sarvesam
jivanam tasmai brahmanandatmane namah

Salutations to that reality in which all the elements, and all the animate and inanimate beings shine as if they have an independent existence, and in which they exist for a time and into which they merge.

Salutations to that consciousness which is the source of the apparently distinct threefold divisions of knower, knowledge and known, seer, sight and seen, doer, doing and deed.

Salutations to that bliss absolute (the ocean of bliss) which is the life of all beings whose happiness and unfoldment is derived from the shower of spray from the ocean of bliss.

Preface

The Yoga Vasistha is a classic text, the contents of which have intrigued scholars and seekers for centuries, and will continue to do so till time stands still. Why is this so? Because Truth is eternal, ever new, ever exciting. It is the thrill of discovery that spurs the investigator to delve deeper and open new avenues for exploration. The pages of a text such as the Yoga Vasistha offer one just such an adventure. Each phrase, each word, when studied carefully, explodes in moments of attuned insight, to uncover new aspects of Truth.

Truth knows no language or location. Hence the same revelations are disclosed by thinkers from east and west alike, expressed in the language and idiom of their native land and generation. This has been emphasised in the famous Vedic statement: "Truth is One, but sages call It by various names." It has also been illustrated clearly by H.H. Swami Nisreyasananda in his enlightening Afterword to this book. Swami Nisreyasananda is a modern-day Sage Vasistha, for whom Swami Venkatesananda had the deepest love, respect and reverence. We are honoured and blessed to have received an afterword from him.

This small book is a compilation and distillation of lectures delivered by H.H. Swami Venkatesananda at various venues over the years. The major part of the material comprising this volume is hitherto unpublished, whilst some of the writing has appeared in two small booklets: The Apparent Reality, published by The Chiltern Yoga Trust

(South Africa) and <u>Beyond Time and Space</u>, published by The Chiltern Yoga Trust (Australia). The lectures capture the essence of Vasistha's message, lucidly expounded in Swamiji's characteristically vibrant and erudite style. Swamiji highlights Sage Vasistha's teachings sometimes from a rather unusual angle, so that conventional ideas become shattered and the mind is thrown into a deeper dimension where doors are opened to new and deeper realms of discovery and understanding.

We hope that a study of this book in conjunction with the text of the Yoga Vasistha will grant the reader a vision of the Cosmic Oneness, dancing within all Its multiple reflections.

—*Swami Venkataramani*

Introduction

The Yoga Vasistha is a scripture of great importance but it is perhaps not as well-known in the world as, for instance, the Bhagavad Gita may be. The scripture contains a cosmology which is most modern. It contains theories of physics which are not only nuclear but sub-atomic; and, what is extremely important, it gives a vision that is at the same time both grand and subtle. Recently I was reading a very interesting book titled Lives of a Cell by Lewis Thomas, where he describes the human body in cosmic dimensions, meaning that every cell in this body is an enormous organism within which there are independent organisms, which themselves house other organisms— worlds within worlds. That is just about the basic theory of the Yoga Vasistha. Thomas says that on the basis of his studies, he does not even visualise the earth as an organism. The best view of the world could be that it is one single cell. The Vasistha gives a beautiful story which resembles exactly that. If one has this view, then I think all the division which haunts our vision will disappear. You and I, including the dog, are not only one, but we are all cells—little things within one cell.

The scripture contains wonderful health hints, psychosomatic theories, wonderful instructions for meditation and for worship and beautiful descriptions, if not instructions, concerning warfare. All this and highly romantic stories, too.

However, we are not really concerned with all that. Most of our problems revolve around the questions: What is our life? What am I? What must I do? Why am I here? Some of us at some time or other in our lives reach the point where we feel: "I am living a useless life. What is all this for? I feel so insignificant—like a dry leaf which is wafted in the wind." There arises despair—what St. John of the Cross might have called the dark night of the soul. The responce to this question is the teaching contained in the scripture.

Vasistha declares right in the beginning that the feeling that I am bound psychologically and that I want to get out of this prison is the qualification of one who can profit by study of this text. If the soul experiences this dark night and that soul, craving for light, is exposed to this teaching, it is instantly enlightened.

Why do despair and fear arise in our life? Why do we get attached to anything in this life? Why do we hate anything in this life? All these arise from hope or desire for happiness, for peace of mind. This hope inevitably leads us to its own destruction, leads us to unhappiness. Vasistha says: "Give up all these ideas of running away from this world. Don't even try to examine what this despair is, don't even try to investigate whatever is a passing phenomenon. Don't even let your mind dwell on what has been considered unreal."

There is one verse which is extremely beautiful:

bhramasya jagatasya 'sya jatasya 'kasavarnavat
apunah smaranam manye sadho vismaranam varam

The world is *bhrama*—an appearance, hallucination. Vasistha compares the world-appearance to the blueness of the sky; although there is nothing blue there, if you look at it you will still see blue. This hallucination will continue as long as you continue to look at it and wonder. You have hallucinated this world and you have strengthened this hallucination by constantly thinking about whether it is real or unreal. Vasistha says: "It is better to think of something else."

What is the reality? That which is, is real. The following example occurs quite often in the scripture: there is a bracelet made of gold. Bracelet is a word which we have used conventionally. We also see this as a form and as soon as the form is seen, it generates a concept and a word in the mind. If we dismiss the word and look at the form, we can play a very interesting game: is it gold or is it bracelet? Both. How can only one thing be two? The substance is gold; the reality is gold. It appears in a certain form and convention has given it a name.

If that is clear, everything is clear. For instance, if somebody called me a fool, by reacting to that, I am accepting that I am a fool. The statement had a certain psychological form but the reality of that is nothing but pure consciousness within. Something that happened in the outside world sent me into this ocean of despair. I became afraid and I did not bother to look into it, because I took the external corcumstance as something real. And so my attention was completely and totally directed towards this external experience. If I am not a fool, why should I react to him at all? In such a situation, can I look for the reality? What is the reality of one I call the other person? What is the reality of that body, that mind? At the same time what is the reality that I call *me*, which reacts? Are these two completely separate and independent realities? This dual enquiry has to continue together, not one after the other. The subject and the object have to be looked into together.

A student of the Yoga Vasistha discovers that enlightenment consists of just three steps: there is an appearance; what is the substance behind the appearance? The mind. What is the substance of the mind, and who understands all this? The answer is pure consciousness. In that consciousness you and I, the subject and the object, appear to be divided.

Consciousness, being omnipresent and infinite, manifests (no other word is possible) itself in infinite ways everywhere. It is not possible for this diversity to disappear, but what can and should disappear is seeing it as diverse objects opposed to one another. The infinite remains infinite all the time and the infinite conceives of all this in creation within itself.

A beautiful symbolism is given to us: Vasistha says that this objective creation is like uncut figures in a marble slab—you are a sculptor and you think of the lovely figures you can carve out of it. All those figures exist in it already, potentially. You can visualise one big Buddha or you can visualise hundreds of smaller Buddhas in that one figure of Buddha. That is how this whole world exists.

The world exists not as a reality; the world is a word and there is a psychological form. The psychological form is nothing more than an hallucination which arises in consciousness. Accepting it as an independent reality, we chase one thing and reject something else. All these experiences again form impressions on the mind, strengthening bondage or rather strengthening the idea we have of bondage.

The external world and external circumstances arise in this cosmic consciousness (which you call God); the same consciousness experiences these external circumstances and these are known as subjective experiences, which change—that is all. Realising this you are freed from the delusion of considering these appearances as the reality. Having been freed, says Vasistha, you don't sit idle, you are rejecting that which is the flow of life. Finally Vasistha advises: live in this world as life is lived here, but completely free of all sorrow. Then if you have to weep, weep; if you have to express suffering, express suffering; if you have to express joy and happiness, do so—because you are free.

I have seen only one person who measured that description—my Guru, Swami Sivananda, who was a completely enlightened and liberated person and also totally human. If you went to him with an unhappy story, even before you shed tears you would find tears in his eyes; if you had something joyous to tell him, he was more happy than you were. He was completely uninhibited; free psychologically and spiritually; he was extremely busy—not because he wanted to achieve anything, but because he had realised that achievement or non-achievement are both irrelevant to life.

Your life is not your life. It is part of this cosmic being and whatever that cosmic being decides has to happen. The direct understanding of this is surrender. In order to see this, you must have passed through this despair. You must have come to the direct understanding that what you want to happen, does not happen. If you want something, work for it and if it does happen, Vasistha would say that it is an accidental coincidence. It does not happen all the time and you might notice that more often than not it does not happen. When one sees that, he completely surrenders and at that point he directs his attention towards the source of all these cravings, desires, hopes and anxieties and comes face to face with the mind. He realises that that mind itself is pure consciousness. In it there appears to be conditioned motivations and even that appearance is discarded. That is a life totally free, instantly freed and divine.

—*Swami Venkatesananda*
Zinal, Switzerland, 1977

Wake Up!

What are the scriptures or texts? What is their genesis, and for whom are they intended? The question is very simple but very interesting because the scriptures have been with us for thousands of years, but our life seems to be the same as if the truths did not exist at all, as if we had nothing to go by. What happens to the scripture? Usually it adorns our libraries and is hardly ever looked at.

You might have noticed that whenever people are asked to read from the Bible or some other text, they go to their favourite passage and keep reading that. It is like wearing blinkers. We don't see the whole truth, so the scriptures don't seem to make much of an impact upon us.

So often we hear the truth, but even when it is spoken by a sage, a holy man, a yogi, a buddha, we pay just a nodding compliment to such truth. I have experienced this in India: someone admires the discourse saying: "Oh, it was marvellous, inspiring." It was not supposed to be inspiring, it was supposed to shatter! I have heard such funny remarks after a discourse where the yogi had exposed the evil of wealth, for instance, and the best part of the audience were wealthy people. It did not touch them at all!

Why is it that in spite of all these great sages and their teachings no change has taken place in our lives? We are still trapped on the same merry-go-round. Probably because we have not undergone one fundamental preliminary, and that is an <u>inner</u> awakening. We seem to be externally awake all the time, but inwardly we are fast asleep. We buy these big tomes of scriptures and use them as pillows, hoping that the message will somehow jump out of the covers and into our heads. It does not happen. And when we go to listen to these great men, we are definitely psychologically asleep, and very often even physically asleep!

What is the first and foremost condition or qualification for being a true follower, a true disciple, or for even taking up the study of a scripture seriously? This definition is very beautifully put in that lovely scripture called the Yoga Vasistha. The fundamental requisite is that there should be a clear understanding and realisation that "I am trapped and I would like to be free from this trap." If this is not there then the scriptures and lectures have no effect on us whatsoever. If you have the idea: "I am trapped, but I think I can find the way out", then also there is no awakening. 'I am trapped' means I am trapped in every way, without redemption, without the possibility of an escape.

Take, for instance, the problem of loneliness and boredom. What do we do in order to overcome this boredom or loneliness? We try to escape into something that only confirms that loneliness. We find ourselves a friend (with whom we are unable to relate) and enter into a relationship. So <u>together</u> there is a boredom, <u>together</u> there is a loneliness. Or, we turn on the tape recorder or record player, but that does not take our boredom away. We are masking that boredom, that loneliness, and trying to escape from it. Thus we enter into a deeper, more dangerous and deadly trap. If that is not clear then the inner awakening is not there.

Is it possible to see that whatever we do we are in a trap? Anything that the mind creates <u>is</u> a trap. When there is this inner awakening then we will profit by scriptures and lectures—if we are not totally stupid and not, at the same time, enlightened. These are the qualifications. Totally stupid people have no problem at all, and the enlightened ones have no problem either. You and I, in the middle, are the ones harassed by problems.

Total stupidity takes various forms but one characteristic is the ability to function as if intelligent. These people shy away from asking the right questions and can answer all the wrong questions. They are philosophers who can create a sense of intelligence without being intelligent. What are the right questions? That is the most important factor. "I am trapped wherever and which ever way I look. From morning till night I strive for happiness and I find nothing but unhappiness." The very fact that we continue to strive for happiness shows that we are unhappy. Face it. Whatever we do in order to augment our happiness only destroys it.

And yet intelligent people go on doing this. They want peace of mind and struggle for it. This struggle breaks the mind into several pieces. Then they catch hold of one little piece and think they are peaceful! That is the whole joke. Is that intelligence? Why is it that having understood this sequence of unfortunate events, we still pursue the game?

If it is decided that it is not possible to attain peace of mind or happiness here, give up. Is that possible? No. Something still stirs inside: "I am trapped; it must be possible to get out of this; I would like to get out of this." If this twin aspiration is there and if you are not completely stupid or enlightened, then you can proceed to understand the scriptures. And where the scripture is not meaningful, you can also take the help of a teacher.

In the Katha Upanishad there is a beautiful declaration: *uttishthata jagrata*—wake up! No one else can do this for you. You can be the disciple of God Almighty Himself, but even He will not be able to wake up on your behalf. If you feel hungry, you yourself must eat. The guru is not going to do the eating for you. The guru may indicate to you, but it is your problem. And if you feel it is your problem, then you awaken, and then you are awake to the problem.

Unless you stop blaming others, including yourself, for the state you are in, you are not awake. When you are walking through a tunnel, you see the light in front of you and the light behind you. Even so, when you are in darkness you think you see some light in the past or in the future. It is an absurd pastime.

Therefore, a major qualification for the student of yoga is to realise that no one is responsible for the state you are in. No one can bring about a spiritual awakening in you. Someone can help, anyone can help, but you have to do it. This spiritual awakening is brought about by life itself, but even to be awakened by life, a certain grace and a certain inner alertness is necessary.

Waking up is easy, but to <u>remain</u> awake is not so easy. Those of you who have attempted to wake up early in the morning in order to meditate will appreciate this. You set an alarm clock, it rings and you wake up. But to remain awake after that is not so easy. The mind loves

[3]

to sleep. Why? Because the mind is born of ignorance and therefore it loves sleep and it loves a thick psychological blanket.

Therefore, wake up! That is your problem, your responsibility, not the teacher's. From there on, ever be vigilant. Whenever I use this word 'vigilant', I am reminded of Buddha's famous teaching. In some texts it is said that during one of the Buddha's last sermons, he told his disciples: "Live in this world as you would if you were living in a room with a live cobra at the door." Can you imagine that? If you were in a small single room which had only one door and no windows, nothing to escape by, and you found a cobra sitting by that door in the middle of the night, what would you do? Would you sleep? Would you even nod? How vigilant you would be! Such must be the vigilance of the seeker.

It is possible for us to develop this vigilance if we understand that we are trapped and that whatever we do to get out of this trap leads us into a greater trap. Because the mind arises in ignorance and plays in ignorance, it can only create restlessness and disturb our peace. It may at times generate a feeling of happiness—which is a mere state of confusion. (If you have ever had true happiness for fifteen seconds, why did you give it up? Because it was not happiness at all!) If everything that we did ended in failure, we would stop doing anything. So the mind leads us from one unhappiness to another, and makes us feel sometimes that we are enjoying ourselves. That is the game the mind plays. When this understanding arises, what happens is vigilance.

If you are awake and alert, can you not discover the truth concerning life? With <u>what</u> does one discover the truth? Thought and mind cannot discover the truth because they are born of ignorance. What else do we have? There the questioner comes to an end. We can sit and think, but we have already understood that thinking leads us nowhere. We are awake, we are vigilant, but we do not know what else to do. Where do we go from there? Go to some enlightened person and be enlightened. Awakening is our job, our privilege. Enlightenment is possible with the help of the master. (Otherwise the danger is that we might regard ourselves as enlightened because our mind suggests we are enlightened—another trap.) So the commandment of the Upanishads is: *uttishthata, jagrata*—"awake, remain alert. Go to the enlightened ones and attain enlightenment.

Illustrating this, there is a little story at the very beginning of the Yoga Vasistha:

[4]

We are told that a great sage called Vyasa had a son known as Suka. He is said to have grown into a boy of sixteen at the very moment of birth, and walked away. The old sage Vyasa was very fond of his son and ran after the young man, calling him. This born sage, Suka, did not even answer the father. As the young boy was walking along, the trees responded to the father's call.

Why was it so? Because this young sage had identified himself with the entire universe.

Such a born sage was instructed in the *atma jnana*, self knowledge, by his father, the sage. The boy himself had studied the scriptures and as his father was explaining to him, he thought: 'I know this already.' So he said to his father: "Father, what is the truth concerning this existence? What is the truth concerning this life? I feel that there is a cosmic oneness, and we are all so many." The father said: 'Yes, that seems to be right and that is what the scriptures also say. It looks as though your own understanding points in the same direction.'

Incidentally, there is an axiom: you cannot educate your own husband, wife or children—they will not listen to you.

The old man realised this problem and said: "My son, this is all I know; but there is no end to knowledge. It is better to have your realisation confirmed by an enlightened being, an enlightened sage. Only then will this little shadow of doubt that has arisen in your mind and which has made you come to me with this question, be completely dispelled. If you want to attain supreme enlightenment, I would recommend that you go to an enlightened monarch called Janaka. He will teach you further and will be able to help you to confirm your realisation."

The young boy went to Janaka's palace, stood outside the palace gates and announced through a messenger that Suka, the son of Vyasa, was there seeking his blessings. Janaka heard this but gave no response, no welcome. Instead, he asked his scavengers to dump all the garbage on the boy's head and subject him to every type of indignity. This boy stood there, unmoved. "I have come to learn from this emperor, who is also a sage, and that is all. I am not interested in anything else."

That is what is called concentration; that is called dedication; that is called faith, enthusiasm.

At the end of one week the emperor had him brought into the palace. There was dance, drama, music and so on, and he was bathed in perfumed water. There again, he remained unmoved. "I have come to see the emperor to attain *atma jnana.*"

This is called vigilance. Why is this vigilance so important? Because it is a sign of the recognition that all that is produced by the mind is bondage, whether it looks good or bad.

Eventually, after the end of the second week, Suka was ushered into the royal presence and the emperor said: "You shine like an enlightened being who knows already. What do you want me to say?" The young man replied: "Sir, my father said such and such, this is how I felt, and this is what the scriptures say..." The emperor responded: "Correct! I say exactly the same thing. Now, go!"

Thus, at the end of two weeks of torture, what Suka had himself realised, and what he had learned from his father and from the scriptures, was confirmed by the enlightened person. What comes from the lips of the enlightened person is not a product of the mind, and is therefore acceptable. This is the process of enlightenment, and if we adopt this method it is possible that our quest also might become fruitful.

A Song of Sorrow

Just as in the case of the Bhagavad Gita, in the Yoga Vasistha teaching there is also a background story. It is a story within a story—very much like the Arabian Nights. It is the story of Rama; and it is the belief of some people that Rama was an incarnation of God. Whether or not you believe in some sort of incarnation of God or manifestation of divine being is up to you, but you can translate it in your own mind as some sort of a super-personality. Even in India there is heated controversy about the incarnation of God. However, this much is important to bear in mind: here we are presented, as the prime character in the drama, with someone who is almost universally accepted as a superior man, prophet or God incarnate.

This incarnate divinity, Rama, was the beloved son of an emperor called Dasaratha. He was growing up in sheltered luxury. This is factor number one: if you are born with a silver spoon in the mouth, as they say, in a palace, surrounded by luxury from the first day you begin to breathe, it is all totally wasted upon you. You don't appreciate it. But although he was brought up in this sheltered luxury, it obviously did not trap or tempt Rama. As all young people wish, at some time or other, he wanted to see the world outside. So he went on a pilgrimage. During the pilgrimage, he obviously must have encountered things other than what he had been brought up on. He must have come face to face with the realities of life, and that set something within him in

[7]

motion...what is life? I am tempted to draw a parallel here with the Buddha story. Like the Buddha, the young man began to respond, not really question, but <u>respond</u> to the realities of life, the misery of life. And so he came back thoroughly disillusioned and promptly secluded himself in what we might call a 'mental depression'.

After returning from the pilgrimage, his services were needed by a great sage called Visvamitra. When Visvamitra appeared in the palace, the emperor called for Rama. A chamberlain went to fetch him and reported to the emperor that since the young prince had returned from his pilgrimage he was not cheerful. He looked very depressed and sighed frequently. He no longer took any interest in dance and music. It looked as though something had happened to him, something had begun to stir in him, and that he was neither entirely stupid nor completely enlightened. Therefore he was dangling—neither here nor there.

The emperor sent for the young prince. When he appeared in the court, the royal guru, Vasistha, looked at him and said: "What is wrong with you? Why are you like this?" The first section of the Yoga Vasistha is almost entirely devoted to Rama's vision of life and the world. If you read that alone, you will probably find in it highly inspiring truth, stated in the most brilliant way. Rama examines each aspect of life: birth, childhood, youth, old age and death and points out how ridiculous our view of life as something enjoyable is. He says: "You feel happy to be alive or to think that you are alive because you are not examining." It was not only Rama who said so; Socrates is also supposed to have said that the unexamined life is not worth living. We go through life totally blindly not examining anything at all, not knowing where we are going, what is happening to us, what the world is or what life is.

You must have seen a beautiful waterfall. Have you taken the trouble to walk a few paces away from the waterfall towards the source? How placidly and peacefully the water flows; yet a few minutes later there is terrific commotion. Similarly, we do not know what life holds. There is total uncertainty...with one certainty: that all this will come to an end.

Rama looks at this body and says: "What an ungrateful wretch this body is. I feed it, clothe it and scrub it, and one day it will kick me out. Is that why I am feeding it, clothing it?" In this manner he examines every aspect of life: "Have you ever seen a baby, how it lies there crying, so utterly helpless, at the mercy of everybody else? And you do not know whether it is hungry, or in pain or sick. What a miserable condition! Then as a young boy, you divert yourself. You are a slave to everybody else, your elders treat you as if you were nothing. Then you grow into a youth and you think that now at least you are going to enjoy yourself, but that is not true. Boy runs after girl and girl runs after boy, chasing each other, being thrown out, being discarded. Once again, the same heartbeat, the same agony, the same craving. Though you think you are independent, you are a slave to a million desires and cravings. This does not seem to be a very satisfactory state of affairs. And then you know that you are going to grow older. Look at a middle-aged man, he is a picture of misery. He is anxious about his house, he is anxious about his business, he is anxious about his property, he is anxious about everything. Money is anxiety, preserving the money that is made is anxiety, spending it properly is an anxiety and losing it is another anxiety. The whole thing is a mess."

Then Rama comes to the ego. He says: "What a mysterious thing the mind is. It does not seem to exist and yet its hold on me is total." The leaders of the world have been talking a lot about human rights, human dignity and so on. But this is the most undignified approach to life—that we are enslaved by the mind. There is nothing called mind, and yet we are totally enslaved by it. It turns everything upside-down before we can even think of what is happening.

Such are the thoughts of Rama. The text is shocking, but beautiful. As you read it you see it is true, it is undeniable fact. But what is of importance to us is Rama's final confession. He says: "I have examined life. Nothing attracts me any more. Because I have been able to observe all this and to see the vanity of life, the utter futility of looking for peace and happiness, for something stable in this life, I am completely and totally free from all craving to pleasure."

When you and I read these declarations we feel uplifted, highly elevated, thrilled. But the only person who seemed to appreciate the views of Rama, but not quite concur, was the guru. Vasistha was pleased that this awakening had taken place, but not quite pleased because this awakening was not born of a direct vision of the truth. Was he going to argue with Rama about what he had seen? No. He was going to say exactly the same thing but from a different point of view.

In what we regard as 'the ancient days', the teaching was considered secret because if it is imparted to an immature person, it can be misinterpreted and perverted; and, on the other hand, it is a waste of time. Therefore the masters said: "Make it secret"; which means: not secret because I do not want to impart this knowledge or because I want to trade this knowledge, but because it must be imparted only to a person who is qualified to receive it, who is ready for it.

When does such a teaching make sense? When one is mature. That is obvious. When a seed drops onto mature soil, it germinates. Is there a criterion by which I can know whether I am mature or not? Is an immature person or semi-mature person going to admit or realise that he is only semi-mature or immature? Would a totally immature person seek this holy company at all? How does one know when one is really mature and able to respond to this teaching instantly? Obviously, one does not know. It is a circular argument. One waits to see if the teaching takes root—then he is a mature man. When the shoot comes up, only then can one say: "The seed has germinated."

It is one thing to look at this life, to see it as an unending song of sorrow and be depressed by it; it is quite another thing to see sorrow as a fact and be <u>inspired</u> by it. These are two entirely different things. The immature, ignorant mind observes this sorrow and goes under.

When we begin to observe life, it is impossible not to become aware that life is sorrow. Life as we know it and sorrow are synonyms. If one is not observant enough, or if one is unable to see this, he is not alive, he merely exists as a material object. Later on in the Yoga Vasistha the Master comes back again and again to the theme and he says: "If you are unwilling to examine life, or if you engage yourself if the examination of life and you are unable to see the truth, you are a donkey, not a human being."

Clearing the Mist

Can we examine life and find it glorious? There is a story in the Katha Upanishad where a young seeker confronts the God of Death himself and asks for self knowledge. The guru is the God of Death himself and that guru tries to divert the young boy's attention with a bar of chocolate. He says: "Ask for anything—long life, all the enjoyments in life, wealth, dance, music—anything you want I will give you. But do not ask about *atma jnana*—self-knowledge." That young boy says very simply and coolly: "I can have all these, but they are totally useless as long as you, Death, are present. Life is not worth living when I know that all I acquire is going to be abandoned." When I know that all the relationships that I cultivate could be ended with the snap of a finger, the relationships become meaningless. What are we left with?

The wise man, as Patanjali says in the Yoga Sutras, regards everything in the universe, all life, as tainted by sorrow. There are two attitudes concerning this. One leads us into a state of depression and we withdraw from life (if it is possible). Can we withdraw from life?...We can commit suicide. It was Ramana Maharshi who pointed out something very beautiful. He said: "It is the mind that suffers, that sins, that enjoys and that is responsible for all this; but when you become disgusted with it all, you punish something which is totally innocent—your body." We do not punish our mind, we do not punish our ego, we punish something which did not do anything at all. It was merely an instrument, like an overcoat.

The other attitude is what Buddha calls "The Noble Truth of Sorrow". How does sorrow become a noble truth? It becomes a noble truth only if it illumines and ennobles our heart and our very soul. How and when does that happen? When we begin to investigate this whole phenomenon of life, living, activity, relationship, bondage, freedom. We are not worried about whether one is an optimist or a pessimist because both are tainted by mist so there is no clarity. One must get out of that pessi-mist or opti-mist and become a realist. When all these are thoroughly investigated and their truth clearly understood without any mist whatsoever, then we can draw up a big list of the truth that we see. Then there is wisdom; and then the truth becomes noble.

How can I reconcile these two facts: sorrow is inherent in life (and obviously I do not want to be miserable); and, I cannot reject or run away from life which is full of sorrow? The truth concerning sorrow can be understood clearly only if the truth concerning pleasure is understood. We cannot understand what unhappiness means without understanding what happiness means, because unhappiness is merely an extension of happiness. (Write the word happiness and add 'un-' to the beginning.) It is not an entirely unrelated category. When we examine this without getting emotional or sentimental about it, or involved in it, we see quite clearly that the pursuit of happiness itself is unhappiness. It is the pursuit that makes us extend it. As long as we pursue happiness it becomes unhappiness. We would not pursue happiness if we were happy. The very fact that we are pursuing happiness shows that we are unhappy. Face it without running away from it or rationalising it; without saying: "Such is life" or "I cannot bear it"...try.

So, in order to understand sorrow one has to understand pleasure. It is something wonderful. In the Yoga Vasistha you will find contradictory statements often on the same page. The Yoga Vasistha is not intellectual and therefore there is no philosophy in it—in the western sense of the word. If you take philosophy to be purely the love of wisdom, there is plenty in the text, but if you take it as a sort of thesis written to get a doctorate, there is no philosophy in it. There is no food for thought in the Yoga Vasistha; or, if I may put it the other way round, in the Yoga Vasistha there is a lot of poison for thought, which kills your thought, which kills your mind before you proceed two steps.

Vasistha, in the course of his address to his student, Rama, again and again comes back to the fantastic declaration that as long as you are pursuing pleasure there is no enlightenment. The most important word here is pursuit of pleasure. The only way in which one may be able to assess one's own or other peoples' enlightened state is to observe and see if there is pursuit of pleasure. If it is there, it is an intellectual game. You have cultivated your mind, you have the gift of the gab and you can charm people, but there is no enlightenment.

What do we mean by pursuit of pleasure? Here again one has to distinguish between the pure experiencing of pleasure (or if you do not want to call it pleasure, you can call it bliss, delight or some other word), and the pursuit of pleasure. What is the difference? Quite simple: just as life brings in its stream experiences called sorrow, suffering or unhappiness, the same life-stream brings other experiences which may be called delight, happiness, joy, for a very simple reason that one without the other is indistinguishable. We look outside and say it is night only because a few hours ago we saw that it was light and we called that daytime. It is one that enables us to recognise the other.

The wise man who wants to ennoble this fact of sorrow in life, endeavours to understand the mechanics of pleasure, the dynamics of pleasure and what happens. There is a vital difference between pain and pleasure. Pain seems to be almost absolute, ever new: you are never bored with it. Pleasure seems to be relative and pleasure seems to be contaminated: it is not pure. Even when we are enjoying something greatly, there is a sneaking suspicion somewhere: "This is going to come to an end soon...what then?" We do not think like that when we have a headache! When one is happy, one is aware that it is going to change, that it is short-lived.

When we look at something which is very beautiful for the first time—a sunrise or a jacaranda in full bloom—there is an ecstatic exclamation. The jaw drops and we gaze at it. I am sure you have had this experience at some time, in relation to something or the other. If you had been aware and alive at that moment you would have realised that for those few blissful moments thought was suspended. You were alive, you were conscious, you were aware but thought was suspended. Ah...but not for long! Quietly something creeps up: "Ah, it is beautiful. I want it again." It was a gain in the first instance, but when you want it again, it becomes a loss!

This is another of those mysterious axioms in life: why do we want it again? Because it impressed us. Krishna describes this phenomenon in the second chapter of the Bhagavad Gita. When we experience something, if we are impressed by it an impression is formed on the mind and that impression craves for repetition. The impression formed by the first experience clamours for repetition. What is this? Is there a sensitive photographic plate loaded within us that takes the impression? This is the most mysterious, most interesting, absorbing theme for meditation. Because, please remember this, if we are not impressed, an impression will not be formed to be revived later and to clamour for repetition.

So, pursuit of pleasure is dependent upon our being impressed on the first occasion. It is totally dependent upon the carelessness with which we go through the first experience and thus allow an impression to be formed. If somehow we can manage to discover a method by which we enjoy it and experience the greatest delight but refuse to be impressed by it, we have escaped. The whole dynamics of craving disappears. Happiness is still within us but the impression was not formed and therefore there is no craving, there is no pursuit.

I may give you a hint now: one of the ways in which we may be able to assess our own clear understanding of these dynamics is to find an answer to this question—when we are placed in a certain situation where there is pleasure, so we also crave for it in the absence of that object of enjoyment? If we do, it has produced an impression and from there on we are slaves. Once the impression is produced there is what they call *samskara*. *Samskara* means some scar—there is a scar on our psyche which will itch sooner or later and bother us. But if it is possible to avoid this then we can enjoy the object while it is there but do not crave for it in its absence. That is already a great step forward.

The tragedy of this pursuit of pleasure is that we are never happy. It is a tragedy in the sense that all the time we are dreaming of pleasure, we are craving for pleasure, but nothing satisfies us...we are always unhappy. If God is gracious and gives us pleasure whenever we want, we become bored. There is no pleasure anymore.

This applies not only to what is unfortunately known as sense-pleasure, but even to what we call spiritual pleasure. Any pleasure that we have in plenty becomes boring and loses its keenness, loses its edge. I noticed this even in the case of our divine Master. I told you a few moments ago that when you see something beautiful, something glorious, grand, divine, you just stay there with open mouth, open eyes and suspended mind. That is how it was the first day we saw him. I can say this very boldly of nearly everyone who went to the ashram to become his monastic disciple. Everyone had the same experience. In the beginning they came from South Africa, South India, Australia, Canada, and he was taken as a guru, as a swami or as the president of the ashram. But once they were in the ashram, they could see him at any time they liked. Something came in, heaven knows what sort of devil it was. Now that ecstatic delight was gone, gone, gone.

So, pleasure, when it becomes so easily available, is disaster. It becomes disgusting. And when there is pursuit of pleasure, life is unending sorrow. The pleasure that is granted to us becomes worry—we are scared that we are going to lose it again; the pleasure that is not granted to us tantalises us and we do not get it.

"Aha! We have understood. Hereafter we will not pursue pleasure at all. We will pursue sorrow." Some swamis in North India are quite keen on curbing their sense of pleasure. They do not sleep on a soft bed, they wear sack-cloth and ashes and even their food must be tasteless (because if while eating you taste and enjoy it, you are trapped). If you give them some rice and curry which you have spiced to suit your taste, they rinse out the food with water till the last trace of spice is removed. Then they sit and eat it. People are tremendously impressed by this sort of behaviour. But in just three weeks, one can get used it it.

So, it is possible for us to deny pleasure. All that we will discover is that the mind is still looking for pleasure in little things. There is something in the mind that enjoys pleasure. Recognise this. There is something in life, in this universe, that brings varied experiences in the course of its flow, and there is an interaction between the mind and this flow—the flux of life.

This can be recognised only if one understands what is known as 'the world outside'. One has to understand what 'the world outside' means and what mind or the self or the ego means. When the nature of these two is understood then it is possible to live and to experience without being impressed either by pleasure or by pain—to live an enlightened life, participating in all aspects of life. That was the original question: seeing that life is full of sorrow, should I still participate in the activities of the world? Should I still live as everybody else lives? Vasistha's answer is affirmative: "Yes. But live wisely, live an enlightened life."

Who Creates?

If it is clear that pursuit of pleasure is sorrow, then the next step is very easy. Before we go on to that step it is important to understand one vital factor which is: the spiritual truth or reality is essentially beyond description. Whatever is discussed in order to understand it, it still remains outside the reach of the mind and intellect. We do not know why this is so. If we want to find the reason for this it is possible that we will be caught in a circular argument, because language does not cater to the needs of the expression of spiritual truth.

That language does not serve the cause of truth is not difficult to understand. Nothing worthwhile can really be put into words. Peace, love, happiness, joy, delight, health, holiness, divine, God—we merely mouth these words, but the other person, if he is not on the same wavelength and on the same level, does not understand what we are talking about. The meaning of these words cannot be verbalised. No true, serious and profound experience is capable of being verbalised. Therefore we beat about the bush and while going round and round we create images. I guess you have heard this as a joke or as a riddle: happiness is...(and you fill in)...a cigarette, a bar of chocolate, a glass of wine or a girlfriend. So, now your mind has fixed on to this image as if that image was happiness. That image is not happiness. You invented it in order to convey what you mean, in order to express the inexpressible. Familiar images have been concocted by the mind in order to pretend to know what is unknowable—the truth.

The next and most dangerous factor in this series is that the listener's mind invariably translates that inexpressible truth into his own idiom, maybe even using images, and therefore the teaching is completely and totally lost. This, in short, is the problem of knowledge. (If this is very clear to you, you will be tempted to get up and walk away because you realise that the rest of the discussion is a non-starter. The game is lost before it has begun!) Now, the suggestion is: if it is possible, can you and I, as we go on with this discussion, suspend such a translation? Gurudev Swami Sivananda often proclaimed: "Religion is not a matter for discussion at the club table. It is deep, profound inner experience." This inner experience is non-verbal and therefore inexpressible.

I might have told this story on previous occasions but it bears repetition. An extremely poverty-stricken, born-blind beggar took up his residence within the compound of a very wealthy businessman. A few days after he moved in, he heard weeping and wailing in what was the palace. He groped his way into the palace and sure enough the master of the house was seated on the verandah, wailing aloud. The beggar walked up to this patron and said: "Sir, why are you so miserable?"

"My child died this morning."

"Oh, that must be terrible. What happened?"

"He choked while drinking milk."

This poor beggar had never seen or tasted milk in his life, and did not know what it was. "Milk? What is milk?"

In his sorrow and grief the man wanted to get rid of the beggar somehow or the other, and so was giving quick answers: "That white thing."

"Ah, what is white, Sir?"

How do you explain whiteness to a born-blind man? "The colour of the crane."

"Crane? What is crane?" was the next natural question.

The wealthy man bent his arm up and passed the blind beggar's man over it. "This is what a crane looks like."

The beggar said: "No wonder the child died. That would choke anybody!"

That is what happens when you translate a spiritual truth into terms of your own idiom.

I took some time explaining this because there is a very understandable and reasonable fear and objection on the part of the well-meaning orthodox religious teachers in India, that the Yoga Vasistha should not be taught or discussed at all in public; that it is dangerous to do so. Why? For an obvious and simple reason. The human mind, constituted as it is and loaded with impurity, is likely to get hold of the wrong end of the stick and come to grief. There is a very beautiful expression in Sanskrit which says that if a teacher or guru declares "All this is God" to unqualified students, the students and the guru will go to hell—because it is possible that when an immature, impure mind listens to such a profound truth it translates that truth into its own terms and quite a lot of perversion may result. One must always bear this caution in mind.

On the other hand, if one is able to suspend this process within oneself, a profound inner change takes place. Truth has that marvellous quality. In the words of the Bible: "The truth shall make you free." In other words, if it does not make you free it is not truth, so search some more.

Now we come back to this business called pursuit of pleasure. Vasistha cautions us again and again and again: enlightenment is not a phenomenal experience or, in modern terms, ego trip. Enlightenment is recognisable only by the total absence of the pursuit of pleasure. When enlightenment arises, pursuit of pleasure ceases. What does it mean? What is pleasure and what pursues this pleasure? Pleasure, very simply, means I and you—a subject and an object. The subject pursues the object and their interaction is the experience of pleasure.

In order to arrive, and only in order to arrive at the very clear understanding of this, Vasistha goes on to describe what is known as creation. If the object can be proved to be nonexistent as an object, then the pusuit of pleasure falls away. As long as one sees an object as an object one cannot help the mind classifying it as the source of pleasure or pain and getting trapped in its own conceptualisation. So Vasistha goes straight to the root of the matter and instead of assuming anything, he says: "Investigate what is an object. Does it exist? Is it a reality?" If the object is a reality then we are trapped in it.

What is it that makes you say that something exists as an object? Your senses. You touch, you see, you smell, you taste, you hear, and what is subject to all these is considered to be an object or an object of thought, or an object even of your dreams. Creation—the world of matter and all beings—is considered to be a tangible object existing apart from 'me'—the subject.

In the Bhagavad Gita, Krishna cautions us: "Be careful with this creation, you do not know what it is. What you see is not what is. This is, of course, the latest scientific discovery. The author of a very fascinating book called The Dancing Wu Li Masters explains this graphically. You cannot know what the world actually is because you are part of this world and every time you make a movement you have disturbed and brought about a change in the total nature or state of the world. So, if every time you make an attempt to know what the world is, you are disturbing its state, how can you ever know the actual state of the world?

If we come down to our interpersonal level, we see this all the time. If you ask a young man what he is thinking, as soon as you ask the question you have set his mind in a state of commotion and you are not going to know what he really feels like, what he really thinks. As you are expressing your sentiments, your feelings, you are already bringing about a change in the other person, so how can you ever know the truth?

"There is a world, sure. There is creation, sure. But what it is, you can never know" says Krishna in the Bhagavad Gita. If you pick up anything you like and consider its composition honestly, you will eventually come to this: I do not know what it is, I do not know who created it, I do not know from where it came. Suddenly your question is answered. I-do-not-know created it, I-do-not-know formed it! This creation is born of ignorance, its appearance is because of ignorance, and it exists in ignorance—"I do not know what it is". To this "I do not know what is", you and I have given conventional names and definitions—form, colour, odour, sound, taste, distance—and called it the world of our objects. It is a fantastic thing and so simple. There is no magic in it. Who created it? I do not know who created it.

Beyond Convention

No one has really understood what birth is, although we know what it means because we have determined what the meaning shall be! Amongst the top-class astrologers in India, for instance, there is an unending controversy as to what constitutes the moment of birth, because according to them half an hour might make a tremendous difference in the horoscope. They have to decide whether the time of birth is when the head emerges (*sirodayam*) or when the body touches the ground (*bhusparsam*). Or it need not be based on these calculations, but on the time or the date when the fœtus quickens. Or is there a moment at which the so-called soul enters the fœtus? If so, who determines it? This was not so serious a controversy until the abortion debate set in. Now it is important to know at which stage the fœtus becomes a living entity—which means birth. The date and time of what used to be called 'birth' is no longer so important.

In one of the Upanishads it is said that the cycle of birth commences when the soul floating around in the atmosphere descends with a rain drop—so that with each incarnation you have the whole Darwinian evolution. As the soul descends to earth it gets absorbed into the minerals (the elements called earth), and as the mineral it gets into the plant and begins to grow. This is the second state of evolution. Then, as vegetable, it gets into man and becomes his energy, and then it is transferred to the woman. Here again you find the whole story of evolution taking place. Within the uterus it is a fish (a little swimming animal) and when it is delivered it is a sort of four-legged creature for some time. Slowly it tries to get up, to evolve.

What is birth? We do not know but we have evolved theories, dogmas and doctrines to suit our convenience. If you examine these theories without prejudice you will discover that they have been tailored to suit what you and I call our 'culture'. In what is known as western culture especially, form-filling plays a vital part. It is then turned into a rule or law. The date of birth is extremely important for filling in forms (e.g., the birth certificate). To the oriental the time of birth is more important for casting the horoscope.

The international dateline cuts through the Fiji islands, but if you look at a world map, you will see that the dateline is deflected in a curve to avoid the islands, thus saving the inhabitants the embarassment of perhaps even having their house span the dateline, with two separate dates under one roof. If the dateline is seen as a very convenient convention then we are able to see our other conveniences for what they are. When all our doctrines are unmasked we are in a position to see the truth. As long as you are committed to a thing called a dateline as if it is the eternal truth you are not even ready to investigate the truth. In the same way we are manipulating this thing called 'birth' without understanding that it is a convention which the human intelligence has invented without any reference whatsoever to the truth concerning it.

At the other end of the spectrum is the thing called death. The yogis state that even in a dead body there is life, because activity is not possible where there is no life, no movement of energy. In order to build up this body energy is necessary, and in order to decompose it, energy is necessary, too. Decomposition takes place because of movement of energy (called *dhananjaya*). Without the presence of that vital force the decomposition would not take place. If there is movement of energy in the dead body how can it be dead? This goes right back to the theory that there is absolutely no dead matter in the whole universe. All matter is vibrant with energy. Then what is death? At what stages can it be said that the person is dead? From one point of view this body is dying all the time and being born all the time. From the time we came into the room until now a few billion cells have died and a few billion more have been created: So what is death and when does it actually take place; or, is there a thing called death? Have birth and death merely been invented by the clever human mind in order to make life and form-filling easy?

In the Bhagavad Gita Krishna says: "Just as in the life of an embodied being there is infancy, adolescence, manhood, middle age and old age, even so there is a thing called death." There is a change from one stage to another. None of us look exactly as we did about twenty years ago—gradually, unbeknown to ourselves, we are changing. We are not aware of the tremendous changes that have taken place in our own bodies between twenty years ago and now, and that which lives in the body may or may not undergo the same change. In other words, you may or may not get older and older psychologically to the same degree as you are getting older and older physiologically. It is not necessary to say that this change is growth or decay.

Change in relation to the embodied being is what is known as time. If you could jump out of the earth's orbit for a little while, stand on a satellite thousands of miles away from the earth and look at the whole phenomenon of the earth rotating on its own axis and revolving around the sun, it would be impossible for anyone to convince you that there is a thing called day and night. It would also be impossible for anyone to tell you that there is a span of time known as one year. You would have some idea of time perhaps because you know when you are hungry. The food has been digested, so time must have elapsed—otherwise time has no significance whatsoever. Maybe some changes take place in the body—black hair becomes grey and then white, teeth start falling one by one—but there is absolutely no suggestion to the embodied being that there is a growth or a decay, except to the extent that the embodied being chooses to get involved in the body and takes on what happens to the body as if it is happening to him.

I am reminded of a story about a funny character called Mulla Nasrudin. He was living in a two-storeyed building with his wife. She was working in the kitchen on the ground floor when she heard a noise above her and ran up the stairs. She asked her husband what had happened.

"Nothing," he replied.

"But I heard a big noise, as if you fell down."

"That was nothing," said the Mulla. "My tunic fell down."

"But when a tunic falls down it doesn't make such a noise," said his wife.

"I happened to be inside it then," said Mulla.

So all the changes that take place—conception, birth, childhood, adolescence, adulthood, middle age, old age and what is called death —are relevant to the embodied being only to the extent that that being feels involved in this body-mind complex.

When a person does not feel so involved you can sense two possibilities: either he is in a state of total hallucination, or he is enlightened. From the point of view of normal folk both possibilities appear to be abnormal. (A very clever argument invented by a clever human mind is that anyone who doesn't think like you and me is a fool!) From the point of view of our discussion it means that there is disorientation of this body-mind complex, in that the mind does not feel that it is totally involved in the changes of the body. The intelligence in the body feels freed from the limitations imposed upon it by the body. Or, it does not even feel that the body imposes any limitations upon it!

We have accepted that the body imposes its limitations upon this intelligence, we have accepted that that is the norm, and that when this does not prevail there is abnormality. The yogi, however, does not accept that but sees that in the majority of cases there is confusion between the intelligence that dwells in the body and the body-mind complex—so that we think that what happens to the body happens to me. The person who does not experience this is thought to be a dunce. The yogis say that maybe he is enlightened.

Intelligence, Mind, Matter

When we observe a thing called 'birth' and a thing called 'death', there seems to be some sort of interplay of consciousness and matter. Is consciousness or intelligence involved or bound up with the materiality called the body? Do the pains and pleasures of the body necessarily impinge upon the consciousness dwelling in it? Do the limitations that the body and mind are subject to necessarily influence or affect the intelligence that is embodied? If so, to what extent, and if not, what are the consequences? Do the limitations of the faculties of the body necessarily limit or condition this inner intelligence, or are they two independent entities? If they are related, in what manner are they related? These are the questions. If they can be satisfactorily answered, we are enlightened.

There is matter in the body and matter in between us, matter of various density and composition, and matter in various states of (de)composition. There is matter being composed (as in this body after breakfast) and matter being decomposed, so that in what are called 'material states' there is this constant churning going on. All the things that we pushed into the mouth half an hour ago are being churned within the stomach. Your stomach and your brain look very much like the earth, and strangely enough what is happening to this earth is happening in these two parts of the body. Whatever is thrown on this earth is immediately pulled into the bowels of the earth and churned.

(There it is called manure.) All that garbage is then cycled and thrown up as vegetables. You eat the vegetables, so that recycled garbage becomes your food. Then it goes back again to be churned by the earth—and pushed up, maybe, as beautiful and luscious fruits. What happens in the bowels of the earth is happening in your bowels right now.

This change goes on in infinite points of this universe; not only in your abdomen but in the entrails of even those tiny little germs that inhabit the human body and in the bowels of the little worms that fertilise the earth. If you bestow a thought upon it you will realise that it is a fantastic thing. First there are the bowels of the earth, then these little human bowels and within these human bowels there are millions of cells. This churning goes on within the bowels of those cells. Within those cells also, I believe, there are microorganisms which eat whatever prevails around them, each one digesting the other. So a chain reaction is going on. This process continues with what appears to be matter and it goes on ad infinitum.

The difference between intelligence and materiality seems to be that whereas there is apparent division in materiality, intelligence seems to be indivisable. A girl doesn't look like a man, and a tape recorder is completely dissimilar to both, yet all three are material. Materiality is of various densities—in some places it is very dense, in others not so dense. Even in what is called the space between us, there is matter, but it is not as dense as those two points which we indicate as 'your' body and 'my' body.

All these distinctions seem to be possible at the level of matter, but it does not seem to be possible for intelligence to be so divided. You don't see boundaries for it, or how it can be cut up. Intelligence seems to be indivisable, even as material space is indivisable. Even though one thinks of space as enclosed within walls and a roof, space is not really enclosed: it only appears so. This space in which we are seated existed before the roof was put up and the walls were built. The building of the walls and roof have not changed the character of this space in which we sit, and the space will continue to be when the walls and roof have been pulled down. When even this material space cannot be divided, the intelligence which is subtler than this cannot be divided. There can be no division of any sort within that intelligence, not even a distinction in density.

Firstly we have material space which contains and holds matter. That matter is being churned all the time, like food being churned in your abdomen. Can you for a moment visualise an enormous genie? His abdomen is the earth, and every time he breathes in and out we are given birth to and destroyed, just as the cells in your abdomen are given birth to and destroyed. If you can expand it further you can visualise the whole solar system being churned similarly. There is a beautiful simile given to us in the Katha Upanishad. It says: "You human beings are like a pot of rice being boiled." As the water boils, the grains that are down below come up, and the grains that are up go down—it is completely chaotic, things are being thrown up and things are being pushed down. That is what is happening to us.

Secondly, there is an indwelling consciousness or intelligence that is unchanging, like space. Like space it is indivisable and indestructible. What is the relationship between this intelligence and that churning matter? Is there a relationship at all, and if there is, what is it? Matter is changing places all the time, chaotically, being churned and boiled, but while this is going on why is it that there is the feeling 'I am sitting here and talking', or 'You are sitting there and listening'? How is it that in this chaotic churning there is a sense of identity, this 'I am'? What is that? On what is it based? If it is based on truth, if it is also real, we will have a triple reality—the reality of matter, the reality of intelligence and the reality called 'ego' (or whatever it is). There is a cosmic indivisable intelligence in which there is absolutely no division at all. There is matter, which is concentrated in some places and not so concentrated in others. Then there is that which is regarded as 'me'. Did I become aware of myself because it was a fact already and I merely woke up to that fact? Or is it because I began to think of this as me, that it has become me? And, since I have continued to think of it as me, the idea that it is me is being reinforced each day, so that eventually I have absolutely no doubt that this is me.

Thus, there is intelligence which is indivisible, and materiality which is cosmic but of varying degrees of density. At some point or the other this intelligence reflects momentarily the changing face of matter and there and then it becomes what is know as the personality. That which is reflected seems to be both inside and outside. Is that possible? If you hold a mirror in front of you, you are both inside it and outside it. A whole mountain can be reflected in a small mirror. It is in the mirror and it is out there. (it is quite an astounding optical illusion, if you want to call it so.) So a thing is reflected in that bit of consciousness and the reflection is so realistic that there is no reason not to believe that it is real.

Three categories are beautifully described in the Yoga Vasistha. One is called *chid akasa*, which is pure indivisible cosmic consciousness (or intelligence). The word *akasa* (or space) is used in each description merely because this intelligence shares with known space the characteristic of indivisibility. But in fact it is impossible to put this cosmic intelligence into words—all words are inadequate.

Then you have *chitta akasa*. *Chitta akasa* is space or psychological consciousness, which is the intermediary between pure consciousness and matter (the third category). Matter is reflected in a segment of pure consciousness in such a way that the reflection seems to be at least as real as consciousness or matter. (It is very much like the mirror. When you see a girl walking in the mirror it takes some time before you come to the conclusion that it is only a reflection.) This reflected consciousness is *chitta akasa* (or psychological consciousness). It is different from this pure consciousness only in one very important respect: it is not as indivisible or as absolute as pure consciousness because it is fragmented consciousness in which matter is reflected. It is circumscribed and limited, and because of its limitation it picks up a limited area of matter reflected in a limited way, and thinks it is limited.

We will pursue this thought one more step. The mirror is a very funny phenomenon. I may hold the mirror in front of you because I want to see your face reflected in it. When I change my mind I just have to turn it and it reflects <u>her</u> face and your face is not there—there is no trace of it. It is as if your face was never in it. There is a second factor which is even more intriguing. You have never seen a mirror, you have only seen reflections—because the moment you look at it you see something reflected in it. You have seen a blackboard or a piece of glass, but not a mirror. The 'mirror' does not have a reality of its own, it does not really exist. (Now you have understood all the Yoga Vasistha!) Even so, this consciousness which reflects matter is fragmented consciousness, which does not have a reality of its own.

When you enquire into the true nature of this fragmented consciousness (*chitta akasa* or psychological consciousness), it is like wiping the mirror clean on both sides. You see glass which is absolutely transparent. The beauty of absolutely transparent glass is that you may not even be aware of its existence. Similarly, when the truth concerning the psychological consciousness is enquired into, it is seen not to exist. What exists is intelligence, consciousness. When that happens, you are in ecstasy. You think you have seen God. That which you saw before in the reflected consciousness (or psychological consciousness) has suddenly gone, leaving the reality undisturbed.

These three categories must be remembered. There is cosmic intelligence in which what appears to be matter is floating chaotically—denser in one place, not so dense in another. As these changes go on there are reflected fragmentarily in the mirror of this cosmic intelligence. That reflection assumes to itself an independent reality called psychological consciousness—or what you call the individual, the personality, the mind or ego. All that is needed for a dramatic change to take place is for this fragmentary consciousness to turn and reflect something else, and immediately something else happens—which you call birth and death. Nothing really happens. The intelligence is still there and the matter also is still there.

A Blend of Experiences

Some of the theories we have been discussing are 'way out' because we have been brought up on a different diet. Just as the body is largely the processed food that we have eaten, our minds are almost entirely moulded by the intellectual diet we have had right from childhood. Therefore in order to bring these theories closer to our comprehension, the Master weaves some stories around them. As you listen to these stories that illustrate the truth or the theory, you have to remember that no example, analogy or illustration is totally applicable. When you say: "He looks like somebody else", you are only pointing out certain features, not others. Only in those features is there a resemblance. Obviously there are other features in which there is no resemblance at all.

As we go on listening to the stories we must allow the established viewpoint to move out and a new viewpoint to arise, exactly like the mirror. When you move the mirror suddenly you find the reflection of your face disappearing and something else appearing. In exactly the same way, the viewpoint you have been accustomed to seeing has gone and something else takes its place. Is that the truth or is this the truth? Neither. That is one point of view, this is another point of view. You cannot see from all points of view, nor can you 'step into another's shoes and understand the problem.' You are you, and I am I, for as long as that ego exists and this ego exists. It is impossible for you to understand me totally and it is impossible for you to drop your point of view and adopt my point of view. What is possible, however, is that you can understand that this is one point of view and the other fellow has another point of view. If you can understand that what you have clung to as the only truth is not the truth, but a point of view, you have solved your problem, my problem, everybody's problem—by preventing a problem from arising. That is all you can and need do. We can certainly understand the other person in this limited fashion.

When we are listening to these stories the Master merely endeavours to awaken the understanding in us that there are other points of view. It is perhaps possible for you, while clearly perceiving one point of view, to have a vague idea of the peripheral points of view. So although I do not understand exactly what you are talking about, I sort of understand. The purpose of narrating and listening to stories illustrating these theories or truths is to knock out established notions (or prejudices, if you want to call them by their proper name) and generate a feeling within oneself that there are other facets of the truth which need to be investigated.

Let us consider the following story from the Yoga Vasistha:

> Once upon a time there was a wonderful king called Padma who had a beautiful wife called Lila. They lived in an ideal state of domestic harmony and love. They were like one soul living in two bodies. If a thought arose in him, she reflected it. If he was happy, she blossomed; but if he was angry, she did not also become angry and retaliate, but pretended to be afraid. So, in every way they were complementary to each other. In all activities they were one, and they shared all the pleasures and delights of life.

One day Lila noticed a couple of grey hairs in her husband's beard and began to wonder: "After all this bliss we are going to die. How terrible. Why shouldn't we live forever?" So she asked a few wise men: "Tell me of a mantra or ritual which can bestow immortality upon the two of us, so that we can live forever in our blissful state." Now comes the first shock of the story. The mystics told her that physical immortality was one of the things which could not be achieved.

What I am about to say now is not part of the story, but part of the scripture. Who determines that a rock shall be solid and that water shall be liquid? Who determines that a tree should grow up and the roots should grow down? In other words, who or what determines what element is going to be what? Some of these natural and physical laws seem to be inviolable. To what extent are they fixed and to what extent are they changeable? (These questions are answered elsewhere in the Yoga Vasistha, where the Master says: "Someone, whose imaginary and dream creations the whole universe is, conceived of it so.") So there are certain features in the universe, as you and I know it to be, which are beyond our control and which we have no power to alter. When we understand this we understand what is attainable and what is not attainable. When you know that this body cannot be preserved forever but can be kept in good health for some time, you examine the laws concerning health and long life and you try to promote those laws. But, there is no physical immortality. It is very important to remember this before we get into the story because it seems to suggest that you can do everything up to a point.

Queen Lila then reconsidered the position and said: "All right, if my husband and I cannot live forever in these physical bodies, I can still worship Goddess Saraswati and propitiate her." Saraswati was highly pleased and, appearing in front of the queen, asked her what she wanted. The queen, who was very clever and very much in love, said: "When my husband dies, if he dies before me, his soul must not leave this room." This was the first boon. The second boon the queen asked was this: "Whenever I think of you you must come and visit me." Saraswati granted Lila the two boons and disappeared.

In the course of time the king died and Lila was shocked. Such is the nature of grief that she completely forgot the boons she had received from Saraswati. Then she heard a voice: "I promised that his soul would not leave this room. Cover his body with flowers and it won't rot." Lila obeyed. (Now we are getting into a mystic region.) A little later the queen said: "Saraswati, I want to see you." Saraswati said: "I am here, what do you want?" Looking around her, the queen said: "Where is my husband?" The goddess said: "I can show him to you, if you want to see him." The queen said she would like to.

The goddess said: "You know, my dear, it is possible for you to see (or to become aware of) something on a different plane of consciousness only after you have abandoned the present ego."

A beautiful statement. In other words, you can understand another only after you have completely abandoned your ego. (I may be contradicting what I said earlier.) It is only possible for one to understand another when in a state of total love, when, for a few moments, the ego is suspended. You may even experience the other person's pain or pleasure for a few moments, as long as the ego remains suspended.

So, Saraswati said: "Normally you can experience the truth, or another plane, only after abandoning your present ego. But since you have asked for it, I will grant this experience to you."

This reminds us that the transcendental or spiritual experience is a gift of God, not the achievement of the ego. You cannot see God. The vision of God is a gift of God. So meditation is transcendental, but transcendental meditation is not something which you can achieve. It is God's own gift, which has to <u>happen</u>.

One of the reasons why psychoanalysis, psychotherapy or even hypnosis do not really work is because whatever is true on one plane of consciousness is true only there and then, not on another plane. So if you are dreaming, that dream obviously has a significance, but it is meaningful only to the dreamer <u>then</u>. Six hours later you wake up and wonder what it means. It means nothing. The waking ego is completely different from the sleeping ego (in a manner of speaking) so that what the sleeping ego was able to do, the waking ego would not even attempt. So the laws and symbolisms governing dream life are totally different from the laws and symbolisms governing waking life, and the waking person has no clue whatsoever as to the symbolism of the dreamer's dream. You waste your time disturbing your sleep and noting down your dreams. In the same way, it is possible that as a child something might have happened which has left an impression on your psyche. All deeds and all experiences leave impressions on the psyche —that is eventually what makes up the psyche! Just as a single cell, dividing and multiplying, has grown into this huge body, even so a single thought (I-thought) or experience has divided and multiplied, added on and subtracted, to become the psyche. The process is exactly the same. The body started off with a single cell and that has divided and multiplied, but no single cell can still be identified and isolated. None of these things remains in isolation. An experience leaves an impression and is blended with whatever is there already, and the next experience comes along and that again is blended. Nothing remains static, it is constantly churning, so that you cannot possible identify an isolated cause and relate it to what happens now.

There is the argument that there are some shattering events or experiences in your life which stand out in your memory even after thirty or forty years. These memories or impressions remain in isolation, sitting encapsuled, throwing out waves of psychological problems or neuroses. Even if this is accepted, I would suggest that it is impossible for me, in my fifty-ninth year, to recall an experience undergone fifty years ago with the same emotional impact experienced by that experiencer. I cannot be a nine-year-old boy now. I can remember the outstanding experience, but it is not possible to resurrect that experiencer. Even if a hypnotist takes me back in time and resurrects that nine-year-old boy who experienced that experience—so that the whole thing is revived—once the hypnotic state is over I come back to being fifty-nine and that effect is left there. You cannot, through hypnosis, bring that experience over to here, because that is on a different level altogether. What I am now is the result of the sum total of all those experiences, including the shattering experience. What I am now is, and that is the only reality.

The human being continues to be a human being. Why is it that none of these treatments work for long? Why is it that they work for a while in the first place? Vasistha is very fond of the expression 'accidental coincidence'—*kakataliya*. The fruit of a coconut palm is a very heavy nut which is secured to the tree very firmly so that it does not drop accidentally on someone's head. A man was sitting under a tree and looking at a bunch of coconuts. Just then a crow flew into the tree and sat on the bunch, and one fruit fell. The man said: "That crow has very strong claws. It needs a chopper to cut that fruit loose and yet the crow was able to do it!" The truth was that the fruit was about to fall, and the crow happened to alight on it at that moment—that is what is called 'accidental coincidence'.

Vasistha says that everything that happens in this world is accidental coincidence. There is no real cause-and-effect relationship at all. Nothing in this universe is logical. Life is not logical, it is partly psychological and partly biological, but it is not logical at all. If you take the whole thing to its beginning, you are confused. Which came first, the hen or the egg? If God created Adam and Eve and told them specifically to do something and not to do something, why did they violate that? Vasistha would say: "Just accidental coincidence, it so happened."

Happiness, unhappiness, prosperity, adversity, honour, dishonour, all these come floating down life's stream. Some of us, I am sure, can bear witness to this. We have never aimed at unhappiness, but unhappiness comes to us. How did it come? Somebody says karma, somebody says something else. Vasistha says that it is accidental coincidence: it just happens.

The advantage of this theory is that you do not take these passing phenomena too seriously, with the result that your attention is constantly directed towards the reality in all this. Thereby the mind is freed from these fetters of logic. Instead of worrying about all that, trying to resolve an unresolvable conflict, attend to the present. You are bound now—look at it. Don't worry why this happened. If you mind still bothers you: "Why did it happen? Why did I ever get into this mess?"—never mind, it so happened. Accidental coincidence. Now, what must I do? That's it! The mind is immediately freed from the clutches of logic and its cause-and-effect chain, and the path to freedom or liberation shines in the unclouded or undimmed vision.

Find the ego and see how it relates itself to different situations. The ego-consciousness is that in which the thought is firmly planted and well established that I am a man, an Indian, a swami and I am fifty-nine years old. The ego is perhaps exactly like the fœtal development, where there is a single cell which divides and multiplies and becomes a big body. There is a single thought: 'I am the body', which keeps growing and assimilating more and more garbage as it grows ('I am a male body', 'I am an Indian', etc.), exactly as the body grows. The first cell in the fœtal development corresponds to the first thought—'I am a body'. This keeps growing into a personality. It is completely saturated with the thought: 'I am somehow related to this body, I am this body, I am bound up with this body'. Until the consciousness is freed from that bondage, no other experience is possible.

The Image Trap

Goddess Saraswati narrated the following story to the queen:

Once upon a time there was a holy couple, Vasistha and Arundhati. They were living on a hilltop, a solitary but resplendent place with a blue dome. They lived a very happy and holy life and they had a few children. One day as this holy man was sitting on top of the hill just outside his hermitage preparing for meditation, he saw a king with his royal entourage—elephants, horses and palanquins—march past at the foot of the hill. He looked at this procession and thought: "It must be nice to be a king, to have somebody hold an umbrella over your head, to be carried in a palanquin like that. I hope one day I will be a king." Then he entered into meditation. He used to think about it now and then and wish he were a king instead of a hermit, until eventually he became old and died.

The components constituting that physical body decomposed, but what happened to <u>him</u>? Who was he? What was he? Body? Consciousness? Mind or personality? The body and the *indriyas* (or senses) limit the comprehension of this intelligence like a lens or a filtre, and that limitation takes the form of time and space. Thought creates time and space, becomes these and functions in their framework. I suggest that the 'me' is nothing but the first two letters of the word 'memory'.

There is nothing called me. Where is memory and what is it? How does it function? We don't know. The memory is there, and when the body decomposes what remains is memory. That is what you call 'me' or the personality.

When the body of the sage fell, the memory was still sitting there, in a manner of speaking. What is sitting, what is standing? What is there, what is here? What is then and what is now? All these words have suddenly lost their significance once the measuring tape (your mind, senses and the body) has gone. But with our measuring tape now, we are measuring the sage, and so we talk of him as still being seated on top of the hill with the blue dome. And since the 'him' is memory now, the content of that memory is "Oh, it would be nice to be a king with all his regalia." Because of this the sage reincarnated as a king. The wish became the germinating seed. Just as one single ferti-lised ovum begins to multiply and becomes this huge body, even so a single thought-seed multiplies and becomes a personality. This hap-pened in the case of the sage, and he became a king. His wife also died in the meantime and she became the queen.

> The goddess suddenly revealed that that holy man was Lila's husband, the king, and that the holy man's wife was Lila, the queen.

The queen asked again: "Can I see the holy man's place?" The goddess said: "Yes, of course you can. Normally you cannot, because as long as you are bound by the ego you cannot experience two states together."

If you are able to acquire the faculty of being able to see on a certain dimension you can see all those things which exist on that dimension. Now that your vision is conditioned by human limitations you can only see physical bodies. If you can get out of this human framework and allow the consciousness or awareness to function on a certain different plane or dimension, you can see the other one; and so the queen, by the grace of this goddess, was able to see the cottage on the hill where she and her husband had lived.

The ego is the filtre. Everything in our case is limited by the ego, and therefore we don't even know how to wish so strongly, so purely and powerfully that the wish might become fact, as in the case of this holy man. Why is it that you and I cannot so revolutionise our lives? Why is it so difficult for us, in spite of all those mighty doctrines called 'positive thinking'? If positive thinking is supposed to produce results (and I accept that it is quite possible) then the corollary, according to me, is that we don't even know how to think! A thought which doesn't materialise, therefore, is not a thought, otherwise positive thinking must positively produce results.

An image has no power to act, and what is called the personality is nothing but an image—the reality is elsewhere, beyond the ego. The ego is nothing but a reflection, an image. And therefore, however much this ego struggles, it is unable to produce any result. When the ego is able to surrender itself, or when the ego becomes so intensely curious, so intensely inquisitive that it begins to seek the truth with all its heart and soul, then it hears this message: "Knock and it shall be opened: seek and ye shall find." That is all. Don't pry open the door, but knock until your knuckles are worn off, and it will be opened. The key is on the other side, someone else has got it. By God's grace, when the door opens, that on which a reflection was cast—which was taken to be your personality for the time being—is wiped so perfectly clean that it becomes transparent. Suddenly you see the truth, no longer the reflection. Someone compared the ego with the silver coating on a piece of glass. When the silver coating is there you see only your own face. You see the 'me', the personality, the ego. When that silver is wiped clean you see everything else. You knock, and grace wipes that glass absolutely clean—so that it becomes transparent. Instantly you see everything else. It is then that there is freedom—freedom from that which was 'me' (even to become what I wanted to become).

> The queen was tempted. "Can we see where this holy couple lived?" The goddess said: "They lived exactly here, but in order to reach it we have to traverse a long way."

This sounds confusing because you are still using your own measuring tape, put together by your ego and senses, your training and prejudices. Abandon that. Abandonment of conditioning appears to be traversing psychologically a tremendous distance, a long period of time. We often ask ourselves and others how long it will take for us to attain self-realisation: "How many more thousands of births will I have to take before I reach perfection?" All this is here and now. But this intelligence, even when it starts to move, moves only along its own predetermined direction. However much you struggle you are unable to break that. If you are quite convinced that you have led a vicious life and you are going to hell, "Whatever you do you will go to hell," says Vasistha—which means that when the body decomposes the memory or the 'me' wakes up and says: "My God, I have been a terrible sinner, I must be in hell." And so it creates its own hell and passes through that hell.

Is it possible for me to say: "All this is nonsense, I am going to heaven"? The psychological imprisonment is so strong that you cannot. Once you have bound yourself within this cocoon you are unable to break through. Even when the mind thinks that it can get out of this, it goes through only its own predetermined paths. That is what is called reincarnation. Reincarnation is not a factual thing—getting out of there and slipping into something else—but this 'me' going from one dream to another. "From one dream to the other an incarnation arises," says Vasistha. And yet, while this dream lasts, the wretched thing is absolutely true. Part of the night you are dreaming you are a king, but after some time that dream comes to an end and you dream you are a beggar. Not until you wake up do you realise that both these were only dreams. As long as you were dreaming you were a beggar, you did not say: "Never mind, it is all a dream". While the dream lasts, you suffer.

Until by God's grace (these three words are supremely important) the door to the truth beyond the ego is opened, there is absolutely no way out. We can sit here and talk for another 25,000 years about cosmic consciousness or the infinite being. The mind makes images of even these and those images are powerless to act. When you are discussing the power of positive thinking, there is no positive thinking there. It is only an image created by the mind of something called 'positive thinking' and therefore it is totally useless. Similarly, when we talk of self-realisation it is an image of self-realisation, and therefore useless. Can we realise that we are utterly trapped in the image-building game of the mind?

In the Yoga Vasistha you might discover a disconcerting feature. In one chapter the author seems to believe in a thing called 'soul' and 'jiva', and even gives a fantastic description of how the jiva came into being. In another chapter he seems to believe in the conscious mind and the subconscious, as well as the ego. Suddenly he ridicules the whole thing and says that none of these is true. Maybe there is a thing called subconscious mind, but as we go on reading and talking about this, what is written or discussed is nothing but an image put together by thought. It has no power or validity whatsoever, it contains no truth whatsoever, except that it is a thought. We can sit and talk about God for the rest of our lives, but that God will be nothing but talk. It is not God. So we first have to become familiar with this measuring tape that we use, become aware that it is a measuring tape, recognise that it is thought that has put it together and thus abandon it as reality.

Can you abandon this? When you abandon it, another measuring tape appears, equally bad, equally dangerous—also it is new, so it is probably clean and scented. Can you recognise that and refuse to pick it up? What happens to you then? Probably people will think that you are crazy, or maybe something else will arise—something pure, a gift from God. Until then the measuring tape needs unwinding. The memory builds a new personality, a new toy, and thinks it is new. It is not new. The king was not a new phenomenon, he was there already. The sage saw the king and his retinue and that is what created an impression in his mind. That impression became memory and when the body dropped away it became a king. This is how reincarnation takes place.

When the goddess explained all this, the queen asked her: "Can we visit the place where this holy man lived?" Saraswati said: "Yes. Normally it is necessary for you to abandon your ego, but I'll take you."

Then there is a fantastic description. They go further and further; leaving this universe behind, they go to another universe. Suddenly they appear in the holy man's hermitage, and when the queen asks: "Where are we now?" Saraswati replies: "In the same place, in your room."

That is, for a moment I was a king in Europe, then that dream came to an end and the dream that I am a beggar in a village in South India arose. Where is this village and where was the palace in Europe? It is all in exactly the same place, under my blanket!

Beyond Time and Space

The holy man, wishing to be a king, became a king when the body was discarded. That germ of an idea "I wish I were a king" formed the seed which began to sprout. Then, by repeatedly entertaining the same idea, it assumed the strength and stature of reality. Why shouldn't we do it now and say, for instance, "I am Buddha"? All right, you have planted the seed; that is one seed. From now on it has got to germinate, so be careful that you don't disturb it. If you ask any medical scientist or gynæcologist he will tell you that once the first cell splits and starts multiplying the attention—or whatever it is that builds this fœtus—is undeflected. All the nine months that which was building the fœtus was at it twenty-four hours a day. It didn't have a coffee break or take time off to go to the movies. Even so, can you sit down here and say: "I am the Buddha"? If you know how to plant the seed at the right spot, it must begin to germinate. From now until you are delivered as the Buddha you should be Buddha twenty-four hours of the day. Then I am sure you will become Buddha!

This is what we don't really concede—we think that what we think is thought, but it is not so. The mind is not what we think it is, the mind is what thinks—so the disgusting, shameful truth is that we don't even know how to think, otherwise our thoughts would materialise.

One can see this happening, but unfortunately even in our own life we don't have persistence or concentrated attention. We do something and it does not seem to work, so we try something else for three months and that does not work either. This way you will do nothing at all. (If we had voluntary control over forming the fœtus, the result would be most haphazard!) That germ of a thought must keep on and on until it becomes what it is.

How was the first man made? The Yoga Vasistha provides a non-sensical answer—the only answer that is possible: "It just happened to be so, accidentally." Why did I become I? It just happened to be so. In this chaotic churning of matter, consciousness entered, and here a thought arose 'I am a human being' and there a thought arose 'I am a cow'. Here a thought arose 'I am a building' and there a thought arose 'I am water'. That is all. Don't ask why: it was accidental coincidence. So the first creation (if one could visualise a thing called first creation) just happened.

That holy man on top of the hill, if he was the first creation, just happened. The infinite consciousness at that point of physical space thought 'I am a holy man sitting on top of the hill', so he became a holy man sitting on top of the hill. Later, when he was attracted by the sight of the king and his regalia, this thought 'I wish I were a king' began to germinate within him and when the body dropped he became the king. By persistently holding on to that thought he experienced it as reality. (This is an extraordinary, beautiful and simple truth.)

There are two ways of phrasing a statement. One way it is difficult to grasp, the other way it is easy. I'll give it to you both ways. One is: "As you think so you become". If you persistently think you are a man, you become a human being. But there is a sneaking suspicion or doubt: "Can I become something else by thinking otherwise?" So leave that phraseology alone. The other is: "When you are a human being, you persistently think you are a human being." Watch carefully now. I am saying the same thing in different words. Is it possible for you to think you are a dog? No, and therefore you don't become a dog. Where does this thought or germ 'I am a human being' arise and persist? It is perhaps as difficult to discover this as it is to discover at the age of fifty-nine (with several hundred billion cells in the body) which was the original cell that was fertilised fifty-nine years, eight and a half months ago. One of these several billion cells is that one. If you can find that, twist it and make it feel: "No, I am not a human being, I am a cow", instantly you will become a cow!

So let us not use these phrases such as "As you think, so you become" as if they are commonplace. You sit and think "I am Buddha. But what about my coffee break?" It does not work that way. But it does work another way. In the case of an enlightened person a thought immediately materialises, but most people must work hard at it. You must keep at it, with unwinking vigilance, without letting it go out of focus even for a moment. Then it will happen.

When the queen asked to visit the holy man's abode, the goddess said: "Yes, of course, but it is on a different dimension. In order to visit that hermitage you will have to raise your consciousness to that dimension. Then you can go, not otherwise. The holy man entertained the wish 'I would like to become king', and became your husband the king, not the other way around. So it is, as it were, that the holy man went to sleep and dreamt a dream in which he saw himself as a king, so that you and your husband are the dream creations or the dream creatures of this sleeping holy man. You cannot enter into his consciousness—you are the product of his consciousness."

To put it more simply: if I am looking at the ceiling and day-dreaming about you, you cannot enter into my day-dream, into my imagination. You are there, but still it is impossible for you to get into that dream.

It is so simple and yet it is so intriguing. When you try to express it or clarify your own ideas you nearly go out of your mind, because we are functioning within the framework of the ego-sense. I am firmly committed to the idea that I am Swami Venkatesananda and you are firmly committed to the idea that you are you. We are firmly committed to the idea that we are both completely separate human beings, so that my dream is my dream and your dream is your dream. Even though I may find a part in your dream and you may find a part in my dream, we are still separate, and neither of us can enter into the other's dream. In effect, I am saying that I am your guest but I have no place in your house. Why is it so? Because we are convinced that we are totally independent beings, unrelated to each other—and this barrier cannot be broken.

This barrier cannot be broken because it is not there! This is what the oriental philosopher calls *avidya* (ignorance) or *maya* (illusion). It is not as though 'this' is an illusion. It is not there, and yet I am thoroughly convinced it is there and therefore I cannot get rid of it.

[45]

The difficulty is that the more I struggle to get rid of it, the firmer it becomes established. Therefore we return to a very beautiful expression found both in the Yoga Vasistha and the Bhagavad Gita: "Only grace can help you, nothing else can." The more you struggle, the worse the problem becomes, and yet grace compels you to struggle. It is a strange phenomenon. You struggle and struggle, and if you don't struggle then it means you have not experienced grace. Grace makes you restless, and restlessly struggling against this non-existent obstacle, you despair. You realise that struggle does not get you anywhere and you realise that you cannot help struggling. It is a whole mess. Then suddenly grace reveals, "This is what it is!"

> The goddess and the queen went to the holy man's abode. Everyone there was miserable. The queen (who changed her appearance) asked the son of the holy man: "What happened?" And he said: "Our parents passed away eight days ago and we are inconsolable." The queen blessed the young man and he got over his grief. She was intrigued: "Eight days ago? This goddess said that the holy man became my husband, the king, and we lived as king and queen for seventy years, yet I was this boy's mother. What do you mean eight days ago?" Saraswati smiled and said: "What is time?"

There are innumerable theories of time and a number of them are mentioned in the Yoga Vasistha. But let us look at it from the same point of view that we have adopted so far, i.e., the 'me' or ego-sense being memory. If we examine this thing called memory we realise something fantastic. Time in relation to memory is a much deeper enigma than the relativity theory or fourth dimension. If you observe the relation between memory and time you are puzzled. Time has its own tricks—or, the mind has its own tricks when it deals with time. An unpleasant incident which you want to forget seems to have happened a long time ago, and something which you cherish might have happened ten or fifteen years ago, but it seems as though it happened yesterday.

What is time? Did it happen? When? How? Except the manner in which the mind regards it—as a sort of sequential series of events—what applies to space applies to time also. The brain or the mind has been trained to look upon this as a series—one, two, three—and computes time on the basis of this. (So time is a convenient measure for paying wages, and that is all!)

That holy man sitting on top of the hill entertained the thought, 'I am a king' and he became the king, and as he functioned as a king he became more and more addicted to the idea that he was a king. (It occurs to all of us. We may not be kings and queens, but we are addicted to the idea that we are human beings—New Zealanders or Indians, etc.)

The queen wanted to know: "Where is the king now?" Saraswati said: "I'll show you. He is in the same room All this happened in the same room. The holy man lived in the same room,your husband lived in the same room. He is dead and now he is still ruling the kingdom in the same room."

Space or distance has no sense at all apart from what you think it is. So if you can enter into this imagination or dream called 'you' and the other imagination or dream called 'me' and find the core of this dream, there you might discover that the stuff is the same. The dream entity is different, but the stuff of the dream is the same, and therefore the entity is the same.

As Real as Dream

As we go further into this Lila story, the plot thickens. The whole thing becomes very intriguing if you are curious, and terribly confusing if you are looking for clarity.

After visiting the house on top of the hill which she had occupied in what you and I would call previous incarnations (to them there was no previous or further incarnation, everything was the same), Lila said to the goddess: "It is funny. It is here that I was the holy man's wife, it is here that I was queen and my husband was King Padma, and it is here again that my king, having died, continues to rule the kingdom. It is here and it is now."

Suddenly she was inwardly spiritually awakened, and Saraswati blessed her. Then Lila said: "I remember everything. Since the time I arose as a concept in this infinite consciousness I have been all sorts of things—a dog, an elephant, a celestial, a mountain, a snake, a mosquito and a human being. I have been a vicious creature and I have been very good."

What is tremendously interesting in this catalogue that is given us is that there is absolutely no rhyme, reason, or order in it. If you are looking for order, you are shocked. Until you get reconciled to this, the truth does not emerge.

When we are looking for some sort of an orderly evolution in this phenomenon called life (which includes what we call birth and death), we are looking at it from the librarian's point of view. A librarian wants all these books to be neatly stacked according to their subject—but life may not be like that, and the truth may not be like that. The truth may have its own standards.

This so-called queen, who has passed through so many incarnations, is just a thought. That which thinks 'I am a mosquito' and that which thinks 'I am an elephant' is fundamentally just a thought. The thought identifies itself with some concept 'I am this'. This 'I am this' concept has neither a dimension, weight nor form. So the moment this concept "I am a human being' is formed, this human form emerges from it. As long as that form lasts, this consciousness is somehow unable to think of anything other than that. From the *chid akasa* (this ocean of cosmic consciousness or intelligence), on account of the arising of this thought-form, the *chitta akasa* (or the mind) is formed; and the mind builds around itself—in the physical space—a physical body. Utterly convinced that 'I am this body, I am this mind' it begins to think in terms of that body and that mind, so that the perceptions are limited temporarily to the limitations of the body , and the conceptions are limited to the limitations of the mind. That is assumed for the time being to be real.

You are free, then suddenly you become a husband and then a father, and the mind cannot think in any other way. You seem to have lost the freedom to be otherwise. It is then that the mind starts all sorts of funny notions: "I have to do this, it is my duty, my *dharma*." "Why can't you give up this family and run away?" "But you know, to run away from duty is not right, it is cowardice." All this arises on account of this persistent reaffirmation of 'I am this' and it becomes impossible to see in any other way. That is what is called incarnation. So long as this 'I am this' concept is firmly rooted, it is impossible not to be tied down or limited by that concept until that body disintegrates, or a confusion takes place within and another concept begins to form.

Having been given the opportunity of incarnating as a celestial, did this queen <u>want</u> to become a tiger? Why would she do so? We are all human beings. I am a swami, and according to this catalogue it is quite possible that in the next birth I will be a grasshopper. If my consciousness or 'I am this' concept is totally saturated with the qualities and characteristics of a grasshopper, what else can I become? So if I hop from country to country like this, and keep on thinking all the time:

"Now there are two more hours and I go to Sydney and then I must fly to Perth," and I get used to this sort of living, it is quite possible that I'll become a grasshopper in the next birth! Because these characteristics determine what the nature of the mind (the *chitta akasa*) is going to be once the body disintegrates.

It is the *chitta akasa* that determines what the germ is going to be for the next germination. It may be because of a very strong and intense aspiration, in which case the *chitta akasa* is saturated with that concept or feeling, desire or craving; or, the *chitta akasa* is saturated with a certain characteristic, which again determines what it is going to be in the next birth. That makes it a bit more complicated and a bit more interesting. The possibilities and probabilities are almost infinite. You need not be terribly worried about it, and personally I am totally unconcerned with it. For instance, I look at June's dog—it could have been a swami·in a previous birth and therefore it is enjoying special privileges now! I suppose when I think of the possibility of my becoming a dog in the next birth, it is a bit discomforting. But a dog doesn't remember that it was a swami, that it did something naughty and therefore it became a dog. It is completely and totally reconciled to its dogginess. (Incidentally, as long as you don't compare your present state with your own previous state or with the state of somebody else, you are quite happy. It is only comparison which makes you unhappy.)

In the same way another beautiful truth emerges from this catalogue which is given to us: "I was a dog, an elephant, a celestial, a mosquito." Again we realise the illusoriness of time. A dog has exactly the same number of hours in his day as you and I have, yet it is said that one year of a dog's life is equal to seven years of our life. A dog matures faster, ages and dies sooner. That which says 'I am a dog' has a different idea of time, a different rate of growth. The sun rises and sets on a dog at exactly the same time as on us, yet within this the dog's own time scale is completely different. What does it mean? You can invent any number of words, phrases or mathematical formulæ for that, but you can never visualise or understand it because the mind is absolutely and totally conditioned by the notions 'I am this human body' and 'I am this human being'.

Lila then suggested to the goddess: "Let us go to where my husband is ruling at present." Once again they traversed billions of miles—within the same room—and they descended on the palace. But there was impending tragedy. The palace had been surrounded by enemy forces. The king was in the palace, and he had been ruling for forty years already! The queen said: "This is crazy. The holy man died only eight days ago, and in the meantime my husband and I have been ruling this kingdom for seventy years. The king died yesterday and here we come and find that this king has been ruling for forty years."

By now all time computation has gone completely berserk, so we abandon it. Now there are other problems.

The queen and the goddess went into the palace and there they found the king; and the king had a queen who looked the image of the other queen accompanying the goddess. That is Lila number one and this is Lila number two.

Is it possible for you, without even abandoning your present name, form and appearance, to incarnate somewhere else? It seems to be difficult for us to understand this phenomenon only because (I suggest) we have a confirmed conviction in a thing called a soul. Because you think you are a soul, encapsuled in a mind and overgrown with a body, you find it impossible to believe that this 'a soul' could be here and there at the same time. When this 'a soul' is seen to be non-existent, the problem also disappears and is non-existent.

If you are a total materialist who believes only in the physical body and its reproduction, it is not difficult for you to believe this. It is something that is happening right in front of you. This young man produced this child out of his body: it is a part of him. While he is sitting and listening that child is sleeping nicely; the same body, flesh of his flesh. If that is possible for a physical organism, why is it difficult for us to understand that it is even more possible for the spirit? If you believe that the *chid akasa* is full of intelligence, full of consciousness, full of infinite potentialities, why is it difficult for this *chid akasa* to reproduce itself as many times as necessary? It is happening even now, whether you accept it or not!

There is a special expression in Mahayana Buddhism—"The sons of the Buddha". The implication is that when a person is enlightened it is as if he is the enlightened son of the Buddha. Instead of transmitting a gross, physical seed, a spiritual seed is transmitted and reproduced. Therefore, a proper disciple of the guru can also be a son. *Putraya priya sisyaya*—a beloved disciple is the same as a son, a spiritual son.

So there were two Lilas. The husband of the second Lila (who was the same as the first Lila's dead husband who had been kept embalmed) waged a war against the enemy, and eventually he was killed. The first Lila asked the goddess: "How is it that in spite of the fact that my husband has your blessings he was defeated and killed in battle?" Saraswati gave a very beautiful answer (which is of tremendous importance to us in consolation). She said: "I am the deity or the divinity that confers blessings and boons and which answers devotees' prayers. But, I do nothing at all. This man prays to me and goes away convinced that I have heard his prayer. And since he is convinced that his boon has been granted, and lives as though it has. That is all. I do nothing at all."

In the same way one can see that if you do something vicious you think that God is going to punish you. It is your own conscience, the feeling that you have done something wrong and are going to be punished for it, that <u>itself</u> matures as the punishment. Why do you think that you are so important that God wants to curse you? To me even that is a sign of profound and tremendous arrogance. Are you so important that God should take such notice of you?

Saraswati explained it very beautifully: "All these things become apparent realities because cosmic consciousness has infinite *shakti* (power) latent in it. Cosmic consciousness (or *chit*) is also *shakti*, and therefore the totality is *chit shakti*."

There is consciousness everywhere and *shakti* everywhere. In other words, God is omnipresent and omnipotent at the same time. A thought that arises in consciousness at that level becomes the truth, the reality, because that consciousness which conceives of this idea is reality at that level, not at the superficial level of your mind. Therefore we cannot easily cancel this incarnation or this idea that I am a human being, because 'I am a human being' is an idea that arose in a previous dream-body. You must be able to go beyond the ego-sense in order to get into that dimension, that depth of consciousness where the 'I am this human being' thought has arisen.

For example, this whole body-mind complex thinks 'I am a human being', so the ego-sense at this point implies 'I am this body-mind complex'. But there are billions of little cells in this body, and it is possible that each one of those cells is also endowed with some consciousness and some power. It is possible that the cell also entertains the idea 'I am a vital cell, interested in the job of maintaining the heart'. That is its ego-sense. In order to alter that status it has to transcend its ego-sense, but not my ego-sense. My ego-sense covers the whole thing, over-all, but within that there are smaller, minor ego-senses, millions of them. It is possible, similarly, that this earth has its own ego-sense, so that if it decides to disintegrate now, we are finished. We don't have to die separately.

In order to alter our status we have to overcome this 'ourself', the little ego-sense in which we are trapped individually. Once we have overcome that we are able to become one with the dreamer of the dream whose dream-objects we are. It is a dream within a dream within a dream within a dream. We have to wake up from this dream and realise that we are the dream-objects of this dreamer. That is all. We cannot get any further, because that person has to wake up. That is our difficulty again.

> Thus, this one person conceives of herself as being here and there at the same time. "I'm the Lila here, I'm the Lila there. My husband is lying dead in the palace and now he is ruling the kingdom here, and he is about to die again."

(Now it is more romance than philosophy.) As the battle raged and the king was about to be killed, the second Lila also pleaded with Saraswati: "Please let me be with my husband, let me not be separated from him." Saraswati granted this. The king was killed in a dreadful battle and Saraswati escorted him back to the original body which lay embalmed under a heap of flowers. He got up and saw two wives, both of them looking identical. Then all three of them lived happily ever after.

Such is the story of life, such is the story of birth and such is the story of death. Even after all this gruesome battle and colossal destruction, Vasistha says:

> 'All this is as real as your dream. Whatever happens in this world, happens in somebody's dream." What is the message here? The message is that most of our problems are self-created, created by taking life too seriously. When we realise this, life becomes extremely simple and blissful.

Diversity in Unity

In the Yoga Vasistha as also in the Yoga Sutras, the Master says: "Examine and learn something from your dreams and your sleep." This is not with the intention of analysing them or treating them as prophetic, but merely to look at them, observe and see for ourselves the answer to these two questions: what is the content of the dream, and what was their fuel, what was their energy? The energy was our own and so we saw what we wanted to see; the content was nothing more than our own mind, our own consciousness, our own intelligence, our self.

Were you aware, when you were dreaming, that it was all taking place within you? Of course not. During the progress of the dream, what you saw was considered to be absolutely real. So the Master asks: "Is it possible that what you are seeing now is also of a similar quality?" In other words, is it possible that you are dreaming now?

We live in a long dream, calling it the waking state. This waking state is intensified by creating and projecting relationships, which are not based on truth or fact. All relationship is entirely and totally dependent on one's mind. Outside of that mind there is no relationship. But, having assumed this relationship to be true, and strengthening it by persistently affirming and reaffirming that this is the truth, very soon it seems to be an absolute fact. Even so a long dream might have all the appearances of an absolute truth.

There is a funny story told of a king who persistently and daily dreamed that he was a beggar. That dream continued for twelve hours, from 6 pm to 6 am, till very soon he was entirely confused. From 6 pm to 6 am he was a beggar and from 6 am to 6 pm he was a king. He wondered: "Which is the dreamer? Am I the beggar dreaming from 6 am to 6 pm that I am a king, or am I a king, dreaming from 6 pm to 6 am that I am a beggar?" His ministers and servants tried to convince him that he was the king, but to no avail. Eventually a sage known as Asthavakra was called in. The king asked him this question: "Am I an emperor dreaming that I am a beggar, or am I really a beggar dreaming that I am a king? Which is the truth?" The sage said: "Neither. At night you have one form of dream, and now you are sitting here and dreaming another form of dream."

There are all kinds of beautiful stories to illustrate this simple truth that what we are in may be a long, drawn-out dream. For instance, a statement is made at one stage in the scripture that because we are in that dream, the dream-objects appear to be real, the dream-personalities appear to be real and the dream-situation appears to be real. Because we are still in the process of dreaming a long dream, we are caught in it and as long as we remain caught, that which we think we experience, appears to be experienced as a reality.

Both dream and waking arise from sleep. We enter dream from sleep; and we wake up from sleep. So sleep created dream and sleep created the world. Ignorance is the creator of the world! As we come out of sleep or as we enter into a dream, what we see, we see as a colour; what we hear, we hear as sound; what we smell is called scent; what we taste is called taste; what we touch is called solid . Otherwise there is nothing, nothing at all.

Does the world exist outside of us or do we exist as part of this totality? If we exist as part of this totality, how do we enter into a relationship? How does the other thing become our object? These are the fundamental questions that one should deeply contemplate and arrive at one's own understanding. However, one cannot properly articulate these profound, inexpressible truths or the questions relating to them. What is this universe in which obviously I live, in which obviously all things live, all things exist, in which I and all things are able to think or be aware and function in an intelligent way? What is this universe which exists and which throbs with consciousness?

That which exists and knows it exists is bliss—*satchidananda*. In that there is no defect. In that there is nothing lacking. And yet ignorance of this profound truth gives rise to the perception of an object. This objectivity is inherent in consciousness. Consciousness being consciousness is aware both of itself and of everything else, just as light illumines itself and other things which may form an integral part of the totality of the substance. Therefore, objectivity is, in a manner of speaking, inherent in creation, inherent in awareness itself.

Awareness is always aware of itself and of whatever it conceives of within itself. Example: dream. The dreamer is the dream. The dreamer is all the objects in the dream. And none of these objects that he dreams about is independent of the dreamer. Now we are in trouble. We are caught in this polarisation between unity and diversity, and somehow we think that these two cannot co-exist. We think that if we are talking of unity—the cosmic consciousness, cosmic unity—diversity must disappear. Why? What for? You are the dreamer and in you the dream arises with all its diversity. So, in order to realise that you are still the dreamer, the dream diversity need not disappear. It was never created.

Vasistha gives expression to this in a most beautiful way. The world of diversity can come to an end only if you can prove that it has been created as a diversity. Since there is no such creation why should it disappear? That is a profound statement. The universe is as it is. You are an integral part of this universe. So, living in this world, in this universe of diversity, you may realise that in another dimension there is total oneness. From the correct understanding of that is your own freedom. All of us—the entire universe—are one homogeneous, indivisible totality as consciousness. True. But as dream objects we are all playing our own little games. When that is seen for what it is, pleasure, pain, happiness, unhappiness, you, I and all other things may still be there, but there is no pursuit of pleasure and therefore no experience of sorrow. Till this problem of objectivity is solved and clearly understood, pursuit of pleasure continues and the result is disaster.

Creation is nothing but jugglery, nothing but dream. As a person lying down and dreaming multiplies himself into all those dream-objects, we are multiplying here all the time. Nothing in this universe has greater reality than a dream-object. Just as consciousness (the intelligence of the dreamer) is the dream, it is also the reality of all the characters in that dream. It is all the relationships formed in that dream. It is the essence of all the experiences in the dream. In this long dream that we are experiencing here, also, there is only One. That One itself is reflected in itself as if it were an infinite diversity. It plays its own games, it dreams its own dreams. It enjoys through all. And even though you and I may pretend that we are independent of one another or independent of the totality, we are not. Our reality, our existence, is totally dependent upon that existence. Even that expression is inadequate—it is that existence. Your existence, my existence, is existence which is one and indivisible. When this fact is directly realised—not thought about, not conceptualised—then whatever be the condition that you and I may find ourselves in, we will be in a state of bliss.

The Key to Discovery

When engaged in an enquiry into the nature of the truth concerning the world, oneself, relationship and why the relationship exists, where does the answer come from? In olden days especially, it was usual to insist upon revelation. The truth was always revealed through a divine mystery, a divine dispensation, divine grace. Vasistha has one of the most brilliant responses to this. He says: "What do you know about grace? Nothing. Do you believe in the existence of God who whispers into your ears? Nonsense! Drop it. Did some God serve you dinner, or did your wife or somebody else prepare it and give it to you? Self-effort—that is what counts, nothing else counts. Dismiss all these speculations and enquire into it afresh."

The Master insists upon self-effort, so that one cannot say: "All right, if it has to happen accidentally, it will happen." This doctrine of accidental coincidence is meant to clear mental blocks, first of all. Secondly, it is to stop this guessing game: "This must have a cause, therefore I am sure..." modified into : "I am pretty sure..." modified into: "I guess this is the cause". Then one is on a wild-goose-chase so that the attention is always distracted, diverted, dissipated and meaningful effort is prevented. The Master concedes that if one is to have freedom, one must engage oneself in effort. In order to free oneself, there must necessarily be an understanding of the causal connection, that is, right effort. Why does one look for right effort? Because one knows that from right effort, right results will arise. So, even here, the doctrine of Vasistha is not terribly cut and dried. I love to call it 'neither-nor' philosophy. Does everything happen accidentally? No. Is there a causal connection between A and B? No. Neither this nor that. Be watchful, be vigilant, then it is possible you will understand when this is applicable and when that is applicable. That which is neither-nor is the famous 'middle path', the middle being neither this nor that. But at the same time it should become clear that the middle is both this and that. It is neither this exclusively nor that exclusively, but this middle path takes on the characteristics of both sides.

In all religious ceremonies and rituals there is fire involved somewhere, as an intermediary between the human and the divine. Why is it so? Because fire stands in the middle of the so-called five elements: earth, water, fire, air and space. Since it is in the middle, it is neither gross nor subtle, which means it shares the characteristics of the gross and the subtle. Like earth and water it can be seen, but like air and space it can only be felt but not grasped. Unlike the earth or the water which can be scooped up and thrown away, you can throw the burning substance away, but not the fire. Just as you can move your hand through air and space, so you can move your hand through fire. This fire is somewhere in between. That which is in the middle, on the one hand shares the characteristics of both, and on the other hand it is neither exclusively this nor exclusively that. This is the fundamental secret, the key to the doctrine of Vasistha—neither self-effort nor grace; neither accidental coincidence nor absence of it.

Although the wonderful sage Vasistha insists upon self-effort, there is always the question of freedom of choice: self-effort versus predestination, destiny, karma. How does Vasistha solve this, how does he reconcile it? If you study the scripture carefully, you will be puzzled. A few chapters are devoted entirely to self-effort. Vasistha says: "What is called God and what is called destiny is nonsense. There is nothing called destiny, self-effort is the most important thing." Then let us roll up our sleeves and fight the battle of life... Vasistha says: "No, that is not it. What can you, a puny little human being, do? Everything is pre-determined, everything is destiny." Then you are tempted to turn around to the sage and say: "Please, make up your mind—am I free to act or am I destined to act?" And Vasistha says: "You are destined to feel you are free, and what is called destiny is a choice which you exercised earlier on! You are free, but not free to change your colour, change your shape, change your sex, change your genes. You have already exercised that choice. And so, what you call destiny is nothing but the fruition of your own free will exercised earlier on. All right, now start a new chain-reaction. Plant a seed now which will germinate in its own time, which will bring up its shoot in its own good time." Thus, these two are reconciled.

There is another problem with most of us: am I a free agent or is my life pre-destined absolutely—in which case, what part does divine grace play in it? If divine grace can do nothing, then why should I pray? If divine grace can do nothing then I do not have to pray, I do not have to meditate, what has to happen will happen. Or, can grace veto destiny? How does that work? Can I do something about it? Vasistha says again: "Yes, of course you can do something about it. Grace itself demands that you should do something about it and change your destiny." Thus all the so-called irreconcilables are beauti- fully reconciled in this scripture. At one point something is empha- sised and at another point the direct opposite is emphasised. Then it is pointed out that the two are not opposites, one is the continuation of the other. For instance, you plant a seed and a shoot comes out of it. These are not two unrelated events, the shoot and the whole tree were already contained in that seed, but not as cause and effect.

Did we not start off saying that we must find out if the self exists and what its nature is? Yes. Even that can be understood only through self-effort. The discovery must be yours. When it becomes yours, it is then time to wonder whether that self which made the discovery is real or not. Otherwise one lives in a funny sort of fool's paradise where everything seems to be clear when nothing is clear, where we depend upon words without having exerted ourselves to see if what we are listening to or what we are hearing is correct or incorrect. Therefore, Vasistha insists upon self-effort. Enquire, contemplate as profoundly as it is possible for you at the present moment. The discovery will obviously depend upon your present state of maturity. Never be dis- heartened; and if something seems to be correct to you, good. But keep going.

There is a brilliant and beautiful parallel in the Taittiriya Upanishad. A student asks the master: "Sir, what is the ultimate, supreme truth?" The master replies: "Quite simple—that from which everything has come, that in which everything exists and that into which everything is ultimately resolved. That is the truth. But meditate and you will find it." The student goes into deep meditation and comes up with a brilliant discover—food! We are all born of food, we exist because of food and eventually we are returned to food—the earth. He comes to the master with this answer and the master does not approve or disapprove. He says: "Okay. But meditate still further, still deeper." As the enquiry becomes more and more intense, layer after layer of the truth is revealed in a very different way. Not as a gratuitous gift. It is the intensity of self-effort that makes this discovery possible and what you discover for yourself is something profound and fantastic.

Only when this discovery is made do we have real, true faith. Otherwise the faith that we have is usually just a belief, a big lie, and if somebody touches that belief with a feather, it shatters. Faith is when you engage yourself in intense self-effort. It is then that the truth shines and it is unmistakable.

What about the gurus and scriptures and so on? Are they necessary, are they indispensable, are they useful? As a matter of fact, in the Yoga Vasistha these discussions are minimal because the situation in which the teaching as given is a guru-disciple relationship. The guru, Vasistha, is discoursing particularly to Rama, the disciple, and the others. So the concept of the guru is not ridiculed but there is an insistence upon self-effort and not depending upon somebody or something else. Therefore the Master says: "The teacher and the scripture are not indispensable, but the realisation of the truth is not had without their help"—a double negative. So make use of them in an intelligent way, not subjecting yourself slavishly to them nor arrogating to yourself the ability to do without them.

It is a very intelligent approach if one understands this. Though your effort was inspired by the guru and the scriptures, if it is intelligently directed, there is no blind dependence. Such self-effort enables the truth to be discovered afresh by each one of you. Then true faith arises. But if you accept blindly the conclusion of the teachers or the scriptures as if they are your own, you have done nothing. They are not your truths and therefore they have no validity or strength whatsoever, and you have no faith. If at some stage the conclusion proves to be slightly unreliable, everything comes crashing down and you are lost beneath the debris. However, if the truth was properly and intelligently understood and the discovery made your own, you will probably carry on even if the master has crashed.

Does this self-effort mean that Vasistha, the master, encourages ego-centric activity or ego trips? Not so. The ego thrives only as long as there is no self-effort and no direct discovery of the truth. It is dependence upon some other authority that is real ego. When I say: "I believe this master's teaching, I am a follower of this master", it means I am doing him a favour by joining his family. I am pushing him from behind as if he were an automobile that stalled on the road and without me he would not move. In all that this ego is hidden and it is not examined at all. On a superficial study of the text we are tempted to feel that self-effort is an ego trip. But contrary to what appears to be on the surface, self-effort destroys the ego, whereas blind acceptance or rejection often promotes the ego, keeps it hidden, uninvestigated and therefore blindly confirmed. The ego is made of unexamined, ill-digested half-truths.

We have never bothered to enquire, but we very humbly accepted when somebody told us that we were So-and-so. And, when a man of enlightenment was amidst us, we humbly accepted all his teaching, as if that great master walked on his knees begging us to accept. 'I humbly accept someone's teaching' is an expression of terrible arrogance which the ego thrives on. When things are blindly accepted, the feeling 'I am', and 'I am something quite different from you' persists. This blind notion goes unchallenged throughout our lives.

So we are asked to pursue the enquiry of truth with intense self-effort. Through that self-effort, we begin to enquire into the nature of the world and the nature of the self. When that discovery becomes our own, we suddenly realise that there is nothing our own!

Forever One

If we go back to the questions that we asked ourselves a few minutes ago—what is this world?, who created it?, what is me and what is my relationship with this world?, is there a relationship?—to whom do I ask these questions? The teacher and the scriptures give any numbers of explanations, but these things took place, legendarily or historically, thousands of millions of years ago. So how can I discover these truths now? It is not possible for me to transplant myself into the Garden of Eden and see what went on there. How can I discover the answers to these questions?

It is sufficient to understand that the ultimate origin of the world is shrouded in ignorance. When this ignorance is removed it is possible for one to understand the essence of the universe, perhaps not the origin, but the essence of this creation.

The first objective awareness is, strangely, the awareness of 'I am'. Awareness, being awareness, is capable of becoming aware of itself as if it were different. It is a very beautiful thing which you can experience within yourself any time you like. If you are serious meditators you experience this when you sit and repeat your mantra mentally. You can distinctly hear the mantra being repeated by...? The awareness, being aware of itself, thinks (if one can use a very simple word): that is a swami, or that this is a girl, or a boy, a tree, water, fire... Why all this diversity? That is the nature of the infinite. The infinite manifests itself infinitely in infinite forms. What a beautiful thing it is. All this extremely puzzling variety, blending instantly into one and the same being—the same energy, the same consciousness, the same intelligence, the same creation. Perhaps the same notion in that infinite awareness blows here and there as wind; as earth and water it is both tangible and visible; as fire it clearly seems to have a definite shape and form but it is intangible; as air it can be felt, it has tremendous power but it is totally invisible. So this infinite variety, from the ultimate in grossness to the ultimate in subtlety, is obviously basically one.

Suddenly you look around and experience that we are all one. Not theoretically or mentally, but when you look around, you see the clothes covering bodies made of exactly the same substance—flesh, blood, nerves and filth—all processed vegetables, all exactly the same. We all breathe and we are all alive—exactly the same. (Now you must dissociate yourselves from your personalities, just for fun.) Each one of us thinks exactly the same thing: "I am this body"—four words. Even in this respect we are all one. We all say: "I think I am different from you", so there again, exactly the same ideas and feelings arise in our minds, in our hearts. Consciousness, or awareness, becoming aware of itself, is all this.

And, awareness, becoming aware of itself, begins to entertain thoughts. In order that these thoughts can be made mobile, energy is needed and so thought itself generates energy. That energy begins to expand, so space is born. When thought moves in that space air is created. That is, some energy moves in space and that is called air, gases. Then friction creates fire and water; and eventually the water solidifies into the earth. Finally, by a mysterious interaction of these elements, food is generated, plants are created and, of course, we are created, too, to eat those plants! This is the cycle; this is creation.

Am I outside creation or is that creation outside me? Silly question! I said a few minutes ago that we all have in common this funny state of ignorance: 'I do not know', and 'I think I am this body'. (Once again, lift yourself out of this body for a few moments.) There is no harm in these four words—'I am this body'. But what is it that says so? Surely some sort of awareness. Can this awareness be fragmented, can consciousness be encapsuled and sealed? No. That which says 'I am this body' is not me but that cosmic being. A universal, mysterious but pernicious habit is to confine this I-am-this-body consciousness to this body and say it does not extend beyond this body. It is there that we separate ourselves from the rest of creation which is an impossibility because we are creation, we are an integral part of creation. We cannot run away from it but we think we can because of the other factor—'I do not know'. "I am this body but I do not know who you are, therefore you are different from me."

Ramana Maharshi very beautifully put this in one of his dialogues. He says that the idiot thinks: "I am this body." (I am using this word 'idiot' in its specific Greek sense—a selfish, self-centred person who thinks he alone is right and everyone else is wrong.) He is an encapsuled fool, tightly enclosed in his own foolishness without any possibility of exit whatsoever. That is why he remains a fool. The wise man also uses the same expression, 'I am this body', but he does not confine that consciousness to one body. He knows that in each one of these infinite beings, that very same consciousness also says: "I am this body". That is a very different approach.

Enlightenment or the discovery of the truth depends on our ability to make the discovery that it is the same consciousness which flows through all minds. If the discovery is not made, then we confine our attention to this body, to the personality, and we live in our own little encapsuled fool's paradise in which the 'me' becomes terribly important. When we live such an encapsuled, totally ego-centred life, we feel threatened by everybody else because in our own heart we are hostile. And when we are hostile we always think the other man is hostile.

When there is hostility and conflict between us, we seek security. Then we start loving each other, selectively—I love you so that you will stand by me when I am threatened by him. It is a very funny story which is paradoxically described in the Vedas thus: Living alone (an encapsuled life), one does not enjoy life. One feels lonely and therefore seeks companionship. So a relationship has to be developed. And, when one develops a relationship, one is also frightened. One is frightened of that person, and one is frightened of others. It is a funny thing, isn't it?

The enjoyment of a relationship is not perpetual and unalloyed. It is not absolute but relative and it is contaminated by some kind of fear, some kind of suspicion, some kind of worry. When we are together it seems to be glorious, but that pleasure is not taken in without being adulterated, diluted by the fear that "you are going away; we are going to be separated".

That is when there is attachment. When I am attached to you, I think your company gives me pleasure and therefore you are more a tool to gratify my pleasure. Attachment means: I am quite different from you and I pursue my own pleasure. Basic to this attachment is the feeling that you and I are completely different and separate. Only because we are separate beings is that concept of attachment possible.

As long as this idiotic, totally self-centred life continues, there is no hope of happiness, peace, harmony or even pleasure. There is an undercurrent of fear and frustration all the time. However, when the individual personality is able to stop identifying itself with the rest of the world, it is able to see that it is part of the whole. Not even part of the whole, but intimately one with the whole. That is known as non-attachment.

Non-attachment is not when I keep away from you—then there is no relationship at all. Non-attachment means not coming into contact with anybody. It implies non-division. We are not separated at all and because we are never separated, because we are eternally one, there is no separation and the consequent contact. The problem of coming into contact arises only when we are separated. When that is realised, there is no attachment. I can be here, then you recognise that I am here; I can be thousands of miles away—I am still here; I can be on another planet—I am still here. We are still one because the notion of division has gone. Then you realise that we have forever been one in the infinite consciousness—or, if you want a smaller word—God. That is called non-attachment, that is called love.

Love is the experience or the expression of a perennially existing non-division. The reason why the yogis did not use the word love was because here we assume that it is the relationship between these two people—where there is only one, never two.

Oneness is not the antithesis of duality. What was regarded as the object because the individuality was still there, loses its objectivity in the understanding and realisation that in this cosmic ocean of infinite consciousness we are all floating ripples. 'I' is there, of course 'I' is there. Not 'I am' there, but 'I' is there, as a ripple, as a wave, and 'you' is also there, as another ripple, another wave—the content of one ripple or one wave being exactly the same as the content of another ripple or wave. The shape may be different, the colour may be different, but it is the same water here and the same water there.

I exist as a sort of transparent being and in that total transparency 'I' is reflected in you and 'you' is reflected in me. It is seen that what are called the two of us, are the same. Take the two corners of a sheet of paper. You are one corner, I am another corner—but it is only one piece of paper. The corners cannot be taken off without leaving other corners; the corners cannot be freed from the paper.

Another beautiful expression that occurs again and again in the Yoga Vasistha is: "What is consciousness or God? God is that reality which exists between me and you." So, to come back to the sheet of paper: paper is that which exists between this corner and that corner. But the corners are also included in that paper—it is not as though a corner stands outside the paper. So when it is said that God is that which exists between you and me, it means the whole thing is God. Instead of saying: "I and you" as if we are two completely different entities, it is realised that between us there is God and in Him we are linked together. Then 'you' cease to be an object.

So if it is possible for us boldly to enter into this quest of truth, it is easy for us to discover that we need not enter into any relationship whatsoever because we are already and forever one. There all fear is gone, all sorrow is gone, all ignorance is gone and love is born. Not love in the sense that we usually use the word; it is a profoundly deep and divine love.

Action or Reaction?

The world as pure existence is 'I am'—one cosmic intelligence pulsating with this 'I am'. That 'I am' creates no problem at all because it is not an 'I am' that belongs to you or me. All the billions of 'I-am's' just float in this cosmic being like soap bubbles. There is inside space, outside space; inside air, outside air—indivisible and yet appearing to be dual. The one does not necessarily contradict the other. But when the mind begins to think that if it is indivisible there should be no duality, and if there is duality it is divisible, that is already mischief—a conception, a wrong understanding leading to the delivery of a baby called ignorance. Then this problem has endless ramifications.

That which is indivisible appears to be dual within itself but without entering into a relationship (which is implied in duality). In order to enter into a relationship this duality has to be of a certain nature—I am the subject, you are the object, we are forever and ever independent beings. How does such a relationship-causing duality arise? There is a mighty intelligence that is common to all of us, there is mighty power called *prana* or life-force which is common to all of us, and there is an elemental power called physical matter which is also common to all of us. In this there is no division at all. It is not difficult to understand that two bodies are both composed of the same substance which in a diluted, less dense way is also present between the two bodies. And yet there appears to be division—that body seems to be identifiably different from this body.

We talk of the body as being covered by skin and therefore all that is within the skin is referred to as 'inside' and all that is outside is referred to as 'outside'. The whole thing is nonsense. Is the skin different from the body? The skin is the body too. In the same way it is possible that when we say: "I am surrounded by space", that space also is like an outer skin. Somehow a thing called 'personality' arises in this complex situation and instantly identifies itself with this piece of flesh. Yet it does not always identify itself with what is called another body. (I am very careful here: not always—if it is your wife or your child there is an identification.) How is that personality born? That is what needs some attention.

In Sanskrit there are two words which are really interesting: *ahambhavana* and *ahamkara*. '*Ahambhavana*' is merely the awareness of 'I am', which is common to all creatures. '*Bhava*' is contemplation or feeling or awareness. *Ahambhavana* is just 'I am" consciousness and creates no problem at all because it does not belong to any body or any thing, and does not enter into a dualistic relationship. This 'I am' consciousness is everywhere (even in trees), all the time.

The '*ahamkara*' is a mischief maker. '*Ahamkara*' is when the '*aham*' ('I am') begins to do something. That 'doing' may be experiencing— experiencing and expression. When this 'I am' begins to experience and express, the duality that causes relationship is born.

How is duality born? What creates it? As I mentioned earlier, we don't speculate here and so the Master says: "Observe this whole process within yourself." Every morning there is a new creation and if we observe what happens to us then, we will know how the personality arises. Otherwise we enter into an endless futile speculation of what was the original creation.

If we understand this morning's event of waking up we have clearly understood what happens in any sort of waking up from sleep and how this thing called world issues from that sleep. In sleep the three factors —intelligence, life and physical body—functioned in total harmony without any interruption, without any disruption. It is fantastic. They do not cease to be, but they are in such harmony that there is no thought about it, no movement in that intelligence, in that awareness, which could create a dualistic relationship.

So, how does dualistic relationship arise? As we wake up in the morning, awareness begins to function. This awareness is not confined to us but is spread out in the entire universe. In order to see it has to flow towards an object. That is when the object arises. When we look into the mirror for a few minutes we get so thoroughly absorbed in the reflection that very soon the truth that it is a reflection is lost and it becomes another personality with which we cultivate a relationship.

When the awareness begins to flow in order to experience its own reflection or shadow (which it has forgotten), the senses are formed. Because we want to see, sight comes into being; because we want to hear, hearing comes into being; because we want to smell, the sense of smell comes into being; because we want to touch, the sense of touch comes into being. It is through these senses that we come into contact with the world which we think is outside ourself, just as we thought that the skin was outside the body. These are slight misunderstandings which can be removed if we diligently work at it. As long as one labours under the awareness that the world is outside, that it is an object, that object is bound to be an object of enjoyment and therefore temptation, or an object of sorrow which we reject. And so craving will not go, hope will not cease and sorrow will not cease. It is possible to solve this problem if one contemplates and strives towards a solution.

A certain movement in awareness is what is called the sense of knowledge and a certain other movement is called the sense of action. In Sanskrit these are known as 'indriyas'. These indriyas are the controllers of our whole life and controllers of what is known as this external world and the experiences and the expressions which are our reactions to the experiences. When these indriyas wake up, that is when awareness begins to flow, creating objects of enjoyment or sorrow. The whole thing is so rapid that unless we are extremely vigilant it is very difficult to understand.

The Yoga Vasistha says:

> "Having thought of the world outside the skin as being an outside world, an object, awareness seeks to flow towards it, to touch these objects."

These are the sense-experiences. But where are they experienced? In us, not outside. The experiences of pain, pleasure, happiness, sorrow are in us. Whatever happens in the so-called external world, the experiences are all in us. This extremely simple truth is almost always neglected and therefore we begin to react. That reaction becomes our expression. What reacts? Is it the intelligence or the body or the life-force that reacts? No. If these three fundamental factors could react to the external world then we would also be kicking in our sleep. But when we were fast asleep we didn't love or hate anybody. There was no fear, jealousy or anger. There was only sound sleep. (Sound sleep means sleep with sound—snoring!) Now that we are awake, the reaction comes into being. We are reacting all the time on the basis of the sense experiences. Therefore it is simple to realise that it is the sense experiences gathered by thought that react.

As these sense experiences flow, what is prestigiously known as the personality is born. The word 'prestigious' is not often understood—it means deceptive. The Master might say that the senses in themselves have no power at all. It is the mind, the thought, that gives them power to experience and to express. So the senses in themselves are perhaps not so terrible, but when supported by thought they gain extraordinary power. Because thought registers experiences as pleasant and unpleasant, craving arises instantly. That is what craving, desire, hope and fear are. Where there is no hope there is no fear; where there is no fear there is no hope. Where there is no pleasure there is no pleasure-seeking and there is no sorrow. All our lives we have allowed the senses to take charge of our actions, so our actions then become reactions of the senses.

It is extremely difficult to define the senses. Once I heard Swami Nisreyasananda give a very beautiful definition of them. He said: "That with which you see things in dream is the sense of sight; that with which you hear in dream is the sense of hearing." The eyes and the ears are not the senses, they are the sense organs which can be incapacitated in various ways. The senses are deep within, incomprehensible, and all our actions are determined by these senses. They artificially divide and label these experiences into pain, pleasure, happiness, unhappiness and so on and then begin to seek one and avoid the other. That is the rest of the story of our lives.

It is possible to contemplate this early in the morning when we can see how the personality arises little by little; how suddenly we think that the world is outside us even though we know that during sleep the world was inside us. It is possible to contemplate how the personality pulls itself away from the rest of the world, treating that as an object and itself as the subject and then enters into a relationship so that the real nature of the universe is left unknown, uncared for. We create, modify and manipulate the entire universe with our own thoughts which are the reactions of the sense experiences.

The world which I regarded as outside is reflected and experienced by me within myself, so that I don't know who I am. Fantastic! I don't know who I am because I am merely a whole conglomeration of the sense experiences put together by thought. I don't know who you are because thought tampers with the reality, injecting into the object its own reactions to the experiences. This is the nature of our lives.

Is it possible to cut short this whole drama and say: "Hereafter I want the truth and not all this drama?" Vasistha says it is possible but it is very difficult. It is a lovely verse:

"O Rama! In the great empire known as dreadful hell evil actions roam like mighty elephants in rut. The senses which are responsible for these actions are equipped with a formidable magazine of cravings. Hence these senses are hard to conquer."

What happens if the senses are not conquered and the personality is not dissolved is told to us in a very beautiful story. "Without such illustrations," says Vasistha earlier on, "it is very difficult to grasp a truth which is totally foreign to us."

There was a demon called Sambara who had all sorts of mighty and magic powers with which he harassed the gods and the angels in heaven. They naturally retaliated, and when Sambara was away from town or when he was sleeping they would invade his realm and destroy his army. When the demon found that the gods were retaliating and killing his forces while he was asleep he created three mighty robots—three demons which functioned mechanically, that is, totally egolessly. That is the beauty—they had no personality or will of their own. They had been programmed by this demon and they functioned exactly in accordance with that programme. They were called Dama, Vyala and Kata.

The three demons walked into heaven and all the gods trembled because these demons did not know what fear meant. They were not afraid of death and their minds were not conditioned by previous memory, by ignorance. The gods were being decimated in battle and, harassed in this manner by these three demons, they all waited in deputation upon the Creator, Brahma.

Brahma's advice was fantastic. He said: "Friends, you cannot kill these people. They are invincible because they have no ego, they have no fear. Fear is born of ego; and fear of death is one of the worst forms of ego—that is what makes you run from the battlefield. Where there is no ego-sense a person becomes invincible; but if there is ego-sense in him even a child can knock him down. So every time these three demons come anywhere near you run as fast as you can. Then, as they go on hitting you and being hit by you, slowly all these experiences together will form the ego-sense in them. Then it will be very easy for you to dispose of them."

So the gods played this game for a considerable time till, through persistent experiencing and expressing themselves, i.e., reacting to those experiences, memory was formed, ego-sense was formed in the demons. Then when the gods began to attack, all three demons ran away out of fear.

We were totally fearless when we were asleep but like these three demons, the potentiality of ego formation was only asleep. But for that we are liberated beings in sleep. We have no craving, no fear, no hope, nothing. We are perfectly enlightened but, unfortunately for us, in sleep the ego-sense, memory and so on remain in a potential state so that when we wake up little bubbles are awakened—I am So-and-so, this is my wife, child, mother... These very soon form a mighty, demoniacal personality which from there on is obsessed by fear and that fear gives rise to hope. These two together conspire to create a thing called future.

Our life is normally propelled by the past into the future. For instance, if I had some terrible experience last year so that whenever I remember it I am afraid, from that memory and from that fear arises a hope that it may not arise again in the future. Future is a non-entity created by hope and fear. If there is hope there is always a fear that it will not materialise, but if there is no fear there is no need for hope.

When this ego-sense is put together by thought with the help of various sense experiences, our actions become reaction, determined by these experiences. Therefore we keep reacting to these—running after pleasure, running away from pain. I think it does not need too much explanation to realise that there is one thing common to both—running. We are constantly running so there is no time, no energy, no opportunity even to enjoy the happiness or pleasures that are natural to life, inherent in life. We can enjoy life only if we can stop and take life into both our hands.

We cannot avoid living, because life has to live. We cannot avoid being aware because that is the nature of existence. We do not even need to avoid being embodied because the body does not suffer or enjoy. It is something strange within us called the personality which first limits itself and tears itself away (as if it could) from what it calls the rest of the world. This world then becomes the object of perception. The personality enters into a relationship with those objects, the input from them being regarded as experiences (pleasure, pain, etc.). One's own reaction to all this causes one's karma. So there is an endless chain reaction. How does one break this chain reaction? Where does one go in order to find the way? This we will discuss as we go on.

The Original Blunder

The little story of Dama, Vyala and Kata has one funny moral: these three people (we call them people not demons) created by Sambara and appointed to protect his army behave like robots and robots have no fear, no attraction or repulsion, no likes and dislikes and, what is extremely interesting, they behave precisely according to the way in which they have been programmed. (We are not entering into the desirability or undesirability of this.) That is the egoless state. There is no questioning at all. A dog behaves exactly as a dog is supposed to be have; a tree behaves exactly like a tree is supposed to behave—there is no confusion. The tree gives the same shade whether I sleep under it or somebody else sleeps under it. And, if it has to fall, it will fall. That is perhaps what we mean by the famous expression 'living in accordance with God's will'. Trouble arises when this is interpreted by the mind: "I want to find out what God's will is." The 'I' cannot know God's will. When the ego empties itself, then God's will is done. Thy will be done—not that 'I' should do it.

Awareness is inevitably aware, like light. And this light insight or inner light—illumines itself as well as everything around. If light falls on a mirror, the mirror reflects that light without intending to do so or without wishing it were otherwise. It is spontaneous action of reflection without an egotistic notion that 'I am doing a great favour' or 'I wish I could switch this off'. Awareness is aware of itself and it reflects everything around, just as two mirrors reflect each other almost infinitely when facing each other squarely. We are all reflections of one another like the mirror reflections. Therefore the interaction between two or several beings who are conscious, aware and living inevitably goes on in this universe. This interaction is totally free of ego-sense.

Though I am prepared to say that the trees are enlightened, orthodox people do not accept it. Their contention is that in the trees and the minerals and so on there is a deep darkness of ignorance and in course of time they will also develop ego-sense. But man has this ego-sense developed and he has to find a way out of it. That is, one must pass through the ego-experience, rise above it and find enlightenment. This is the common view. We are full of ego; our ego does not need to be awakened, we have to deal with it.

We saw, according to the story of Dama, Vyala and Kata that it was possible to awaken the ego-sense in these three. How does that happen? How is it possible that I begin to entertain this ego-sense? How does it operate? What exactly is it? How and when does the experiencer come into being? It is the experiencer that seeks a repetition of desirable experiences. If that problem is not there and we live as two mirrors live, merely reflecting each other, being aware of one another's company and doing whatever is appropriate in each situation, then there is no pursuit of pleasure and no sorrow. We enjoy each other's company when we are together and when we are separated there is no problem.

Who is the experiencer of experiences? It is very interesting if we observe this phenomenon within ourselves. The eyes have no discrimination whatsoever—ugly face, beautiful face, saintly face, sinner's face, young face, old face—when the eyes are open they see. As we walk along the road we see very many faces. Of these we hardly remember three—two perhaps. Why is it so? The others were reflected by the eyes without an impression being formed. Where there is no registration, everything is free, but where there is registration there is a problem. Suddenly we see an attractive person. What does that mean? Attractive can mean both very beautiful and very ugly. Both attract attention, both form an impression. That is how the observer arises from a pure interaction of awareness within itself.

There is just one more problem and that is this light of awareness shines illuminating itself and all others. It may even be aware of our faces but since the light shines illuminating itself it does not fall into the error of regarding that as a pure object. Let us go back to the two mirrors now. Just for the sake of argument imagine that you are one of them. It would be very difficult for you, looking into the other mirror, to know which of those infinite reflections is you and which is the reflection of the reflection. In other words, if we had sustained, clear and unclouded understanding that all the experiences we go through during our day are really and truly experiences that take place within us, then our attention will be constantly on the self, on the subject. However, when there is an impressive experience, in some mysterious way, one does not know how this happens, the subject, which is the awareness (not a subject) and is aware of itself and the objects, forgets that the objects are not objects but merely reflections within each other.

If we experiment with this, we might discover that when there is an impressive experience, whether it is pleasant or unpleasant, suddenly something happens—there is an inner self-unawareness. In that inner self-unawareness the object looms very large and suddenly from somewhere there arises a feeling that the object is real as an object and our pleasure comes from that object or our pain comes from that object. It is in this moment of self-unawareness that what is known as the ego is born. Till then there is no ego.

Thus there are two things involved in the arising of the ego: a momentary self-unawareness and, combined with this, the feeling that pleasure or pain comes from an object. When we have decided that pleasure or pain comes from an object and we are the enjoyer or sufferer of that pleasure or pain, we are trapped. From there on it is one continuous rat-race of running after this pleasure and running away from that pain. The impression 'my pleasure comes from that', has been formed and strengthened by repeated assertion in a moment of self-unawareness when the experiencer, the ego, arises. That ego feels threatened that somebody wants to take its happiness away and then it is not prepared to examine this situation afresh. The pursuit of pleasure is so intense that we are not allowed even a moment's respite to reconsider the whole problem. So we go on and on and on.

It is these impressions that are dangerous. They are known in Sanskrit as *samskaras*—scars on our soul, scars on this pure awareness which could otherwise enable us to lead an enlightened life like a Buddha, like a Jesus, like the great ones. These scars, *samskaras* , are formed when the experiencer, which arises and dies a thousand times a second, is made permanent by a single momentary lapse of self-awareness—the original blunder. Just one moment's self-unawareness lengthens the life-span of this momentary experiencer, the ego. Having been born, it accumulates and stores in itself memory after memory (impressions), strengthens itself by gathering all experiences to itself as if it were the sole experiencer and then reacts to external circumstances, external stimuli, as if it were the doer of actions. The fact that the experience of pleasure or pain arises and exists in itself is forgotten. It is the ego that perpetuates this whole show instead of dying at the moment of its birth.

What reacts or responds when we are faced with the challenge of life, it is not the intelligence but the silly little intellectual memories, the scars that have been accumulated with great trouble and at great expense! The intelligence is completely muddled by the responses from these scars. It is not that memory in itself is bad—it may be needed, or it may be useful—but memory as the source of action is dangerous. Memory interferes in, distorts, perverts and destroys our actions, our relationships, or lives. The 'me' or the self is nothing but all these memories, all these *samskaras* put together. It is that that creates a misunderstanding of what is, regarding that as the world so that we are never fresh in our action, in our approach to life.

It seems that George Bernard Shaw was once asked: "Who do you consider the wisest man in the world?" He replied: "My tailor because he is the only one who measures me anew every time he sees me." This is something which we don't do. If I am nice to you you carry that memory and you judge me for all time to come by that memory. If I pick a quarrel with you today you will probably not want to look at me again. I might have changed, I might have become a Buddha, but because of that memory you don't understand. That is very immature, childish behaviour which distorts every action.

If that moment's self-unawareness had not been there, we would have blissfully passed through life without ever being terribly impressed by it one way or the other. That seems a bit dull, but it might not be because there are moments of supreme delight and also suffering granted to us in our own lives. As children I am quite sure we all yelled in joy when we had a chocolate or an ice cream. Also, we have had tummy-aches, headaches, examination aches, heartaches and all sorts of things. But do any of us remember those now? No. Delight was there but it did not produce such a deep impression as to be carried around by us now. Those painful experiences were also not deeply registered and so they have vanished into thin air. So it is possible for us to live a full life of ecstasy, delight and also suffering without the ego-sense—which means without creating an inner registrar to take impressions.

What is <u>is</u>. No sage or seer denies the existence of all this. But the <u>mind</u> tries to understand it on the basis of memory and therefore creates a misunderstanding so there is a misapprehension of all this. If we are able to look with a fresh vision, in the words of the Bible: we shall be like little children in the Kingdom of God. The world of our conception is an optical illusion. Drop the world and look. When we look in that way we will realise that that which looks is not the 'me'—the memory, the scars, the distorted, prejudiced, restless mind. When such a vision arises, that vision does not have an observer, it is pure light. In pure, spontaneous living, enlightened living, there is no ego-sense. We are like the mirror and like the light which function without ego-sense.

Precision Balance

Just as at one particular instant, a moment's self-unawareness brought about the ego, it is possible that at another time something will happen which can remind us of the truth and in a moment of awareness we are shocked into wakefulness. (But then one should be lucky enough to be awake at that moment!) Gurudev Swami Sivananda used to sing: "When you get knocks and blows in the daily battle of life, then your mind is duly turned towards the spiritual path." This is quite true, <u>but</u> (there is a 'big' but here) it does not happen to everybody. When we get knocks and blows, what do we do? We give them back to the person from whom we got them. It needs an inner awakening to bring about an inner awakening. So the master, Vasistha, suggests a few hints. He says: "Inner awakening, enlightenment, liberation or *moksha, nirvana*—whatever you wish to call it—is regarded as a kingdom. There are four gate-keepers or sentinels guarding its four entrances. They are *sama, vichara, santosha, caturthah sadhusangamah.* Try to make friends with them and they will let you in." They will strip you of the ego and then let you enter.

These four are the enemies of this ego-sense, as it were. It is very difficult to translate them, so I will give the dictionary meanings and then we will look into them. *Sama* is tranquility, self-control or control of mind. *Vichara* is usually translated as enquiry but it is a lot more. It implies a mind that is constantly observed. *Santosha* may be taken as contentment, the total absence of craving. And *caturthahsadhusanga-mah*, the fourth, is *satsanga*—company of the wise, the enlightened, the good. Every factor which contributed to the formation of the ego-sense is negated by or destroyed by these four. It is not because we want those factors to be destroyed but in spite of them, the ego will be annihilated if we concentrate upon these four. The Master adds: "If you cannot make friends with all four, then cultivate the friendship of at least one of these and you will realise that all the rest accompany this one." One leads to the other, one involves the other, one embraces the other, one is the same as the other. You cannot have peace of mind if your mind is not restrained or controlled. You cannot have peace of mind if you are not contented. You cannot have peace of mind if the mind is not being observed all the time. And that mind itself is good company. If you have peace within, that is the best company in the world.

Let us now look into each of these four sentinels more deeply. First, *sama*. When the Sanskrit word *sama* is transliterated, it is written *s-a-m-a* and it means just that (if you read the last *-a* as *-e*). Can there be a sameness internally? Can there be an equanimity or a state of inner equilibrium in all conditions, whatever be the external circumstances in which we are placed? *Sama* does not mean that you are absolutely still but it is absence of violent reaction, absence of inner turbulence. *Sama* is a different form of self-control, control of the mind of a different quality, control of the senses of a different quality.

What is self-control or control of the mind? Some of us might have tried to control our minds. What happens? Suddenly the mind becomes our enemy and it seems to be more powerful than we are. Whereas before we started this joke it occasionally seemed to play some mischief, the moment we decided to control it, we were completely under its control. This is the most disgraceful part of human life on earth—we are enslaved by something which we cannot see, which does not seem to exist. It is so subtle and yet its effect on our behaviour, our happiness, our peace and on our life in general is utterly devastating. What is the mind? Nobody knows. Why is it so? Because it is the mind that asks the question. We use water to dilute other things but can we dilute water with water? That is what we are doing when we try to control the mind with mind—diluting water with water.

What does control of mind mean? What does *sama* mean? One needs to work on it with great intensity, with great sincerity, eagerness, tremendous seriousness and also curiosity (and so I have coined a new word, 'seriosity'—neither totally serious nor totally curious, but part of each). Does the mind want to control itself? What for? "I want to surrender my ego to my god or to my guru so that I may be happy in heaven." Good grief! Before we turn round, ego comes the other way and hits us!

So can we force ourselves to control the mind? No. When we force ourselves to do what we do not want to do in reality, we get into a depression. That is what depression means. This inner battle must be resolved. We must make up our minds. If we do not want to do it, drop it; if we want to do it, do it. *Sama* is suppression of thoughts and feelings. If it were, who would be the controller and who the controlled? Suppression is another name for a type of turmoil. In one type one is excited and expressing all the time; in the other, one is excited and suppressing all the time—the excitement being common.

When there is anxiety that one's feelings must be controlled, suppressed or eradicated, one walks into two types of traps. One: we hallucinate or imagine that the mind and the feelings are under perfect control, i.e., we redefine control to suit our imagination. The other trap is worse. When we find that it is difficult to control the mind then we look for exotic methods for controlled it, for example, drugs. These are two main dangers in assuming that control of mind means total suppression of thoughts and feelings.

More sensibly, we might give up the whole thing as useless! We realise that we cannot live with the restless mind nor can we control it; and, the mind dividing itself into the controller and the controlled, the observer and the observed, is pure waste of time! We realise that as long as there is life, there will be motion. Keep it just there, without repressing it, without expressing it. Let life flow on without terrible turmoil and excitement.

This is beautifully described in the Yoga Sutras where three stages are given: 1) The stage when you cultivate self-restraint. You are used to letting yourself go, so pull the reins in, cultivate the habit of restraint (which may even look like suppression), learn to say 'no'. 2) Let this become habitual, so that every time there is an excitement, the habit of self-restraint also comes up. The two jump together. There is certainly some inner conflict at that point. Let this go on until...3) The third stage is reached, where the two become of equal force. This is a beautiful thing.

In the search for truth there must be a certain amount of seriousness, intensity of application, a healthy curiosity and, if you like, cynicism. If we are not cynical we will not get very far in this search for truth because suddenly something might happen which has the external appearance of control and we will succumb there. It is like many animals which, when confronted by great danger, collapse and lie down as if they are dead so that the predator may go away. Then they jump up and run away. When attacked very vehemently the mind can do that too. It can get stupefied so we think: "Ah! I have controlled the mind. It is so still." We are fast asleep—the mind is merely taking rest in order that it can attack us a bit later!

What a fantastic creation this human being is. We are told he is supposed to have free will to do and not to do and therefore he can use his choice and be good, do good. But why is it that God has placed all the most vital physical and physiological functions out of the reach of man's will? I suggest that even God was cynical. While creating us he gave us a sort of illusion that we are free to do what we want to do but, in fact, we have no control over our heart, our lungs, our digestion, our nervous system, nothing. What sort of control do we have? To suck our thumb or not to suck our thumb!

All the good things of life are God's gifts, including what are known as control of mind and peace of mind. The more we struggle to get peace of mind, the farther it will recede. But the lazy person does not deserve these gifts. Therefore we have to work very hard with seriosity and, if you like, cynicism, and when we come to the end of our tether then the mind comes to an end. Control of mind is when the mind comes to a clear understanding of its own total impotence. Then the egoism stands baffled, suspended, stupefied—wondering why it cannot do even the smallest, simplest thing like giving up smoking.

Patanjali and also our master, Swami Sivananda, used to recommend substituting good thoughts for bad thoughts, good feelings for bad feelings. These are socially desirable, acceptable, beneficial. Society likes a good man in preference to a bad man. And in a remote, indirect way the substitution of good thoughts and good feelings for bad thoughts and bad feelings leads one a little closer to true control of mind in as much as wicked thoughts are more turbulent than good thoughts. Good thoughts tend to a little more peacefulness, tranquillity. However, while we are developing these good thoughts we realise that these are also thoughts and they are not under our control. While trying to think these good thoughts, as in meditation, we suddenly realise that unwanted thoughts seems to be more welcome in the mind.

The mantra is a thought. When we are sitting and meditating it is the thought that thinks the mantra, repeats the mantra, and the mantra is made of the substance of the mind. It does not happen in God. While we are struggling to keep the mantra going the mind thinks of all sorts of other thoughts which come freely, smoothly, without any problem. Why is that? Who invited them? The very thoughts that we wish to avoid seem to come more freely than those thoughts which we are struggling to think.

While the uncontrolled mind plays its own games suddenly we realise: "I am unable to deal with this mind and its restlessness. I cannot live with it, yet I seem to be unable to live without it." At that point a certain stillness arises which is really not suppression of any thoughts and feelings, but stillness of a very different quality. It is a stillness that is born of an awakening insight.

When we see no hope at all—"Nothing can be done. Oh my God!"—suddenly the control happens. That is called *sama*. If we reach that stage we will find the mind is controlled. Not that 'I' am controlling the mind, not that the mind is controlling the mind, but the mind is controlled. It can only be phrased in the passive voice. By whom? No idea.

The yogi lives, but for every turbulence there is a counter-turbulence; for every excitement, there is a balancing force; and he ensures that these two are in a state of perfect equilibrium. Then what has to happen happens and what is called 'duty', which is the due perfor mance of what has to happen, takes place. You are not doing anything nor are you refraining from doing it, you are neither pushing nor pulling back. That beautiful balance, the perfect precision balance, is what is called *sama*.

Fuel for the Fire

The second gate-keeper to the kingdom of enlightenment is *vichara* —relentless observation, unblinking vigilance. *Vichara* is the mainstay of the yoga of the Yoga Vasistha. *Vichara* is usually translated as enquiry, but though enquiry suggests an intellectual approach, *vichara* is completely and totally distinct from any intellectual game. It is not psychological analysis, psycho-analysis or mental activity, but a direct, inward observation of everything in life which is very deep, profound and tremendously effective if done properly.

The word is written: *vichara*. The first syllable *vi* in Sanskrit often means just the English word 'very', in the sense efficient, intensified, excellent. The Sanskrit prefix *vi-* is literally 'very good'. *Chara* is the root. In transliteration *char* is written 'c-a-r'. 'Car' in English is the car which moves. Therefore *vichara* is 'very movement' or, in other words, very efficient movement, well-directed movement. *Vichara* has even been translated as reflection. But in reflection there is one defect: if you look at the reflection in a mirror the reflection is static. *Vichara*, on the other hand, is not static. It is movement of consciousness, it is movement of awareness in an efficient, single beam so there is efficient observation, direct observation, undeflected observation.

Vichara is observation without an observer. If the observer is raised in this *vichara*, that becomes the ego. When you say: "I am watching my mind", it means the 'I' thinks that it is watching the mind. When a problem arises in our life we try to solve it by various means: logically, morally, immorally, by hook or by crook or by any other means at our disposal. All this is determined and conditioned by the ego. That ego must come to a conclusion.

Our problems are not logical, and the conclusions cannot be logical either, though they may not go against logic. The ego is born of ignorance and dualism; dualism implies logic and logic implies dualism. The problems of life are not yours alone, they are universal. You may have your own special ones, but problems and sorrow are inherent in life, in living.

As long as we continue to be ignorant, confusion is created. When that is seen the ego does not attempt to solve the problem any more. The 'I' gives up. At that point there is surrender and something else arises. It is not the ego or the self but the intelligence which shines. That intelligence—not the observer but the observation—does the *vichara*. In some classics you might find it described as the 'witness consciousness'. Witness not in the sense that it stands aloof but because it is everywhere—in me, in you, in the chairs and the table. It is not 'I': it is not the limited, fragmented ego.

What is this 'I'? What is this ego? What is this self? How does it arise? This problem confronts us again and again and again. And unless that is grappled with in the practice of yoga, that ego will come up again in some form or other. If, in doing *vichara*, there is the feeling 'I am doing *vichara*', the 'I am' is back on its throne again, and from the throne it will have to be thrown out!

Watch carefully how hypocritical we are when we say: "I am full of ignorance. Oh God, I want to be better". Isn't it another lovely way of saying how good we are? What is this? When we feel 'I want to be good, I want to do good', where does this impulse come from? I want to meditate, I want to obtain self-realisation, liberation. Who is that 'I' who wants to do all this? If you don't know that either you enter into a field of make-believe or you are in total ignorance. We may go on repeating: "I want to be good, I want to be loving, I want to be kind, I want to worship God", yet after awhile we notice that nothing happens, because these words just stay between the throat and the mouth. The same happens to our constant prayer because only our jaws are exercised, nothing happens in our mind. We don't know where those words are produced, or where the ideas that these words symbolise arise and therefore we are not moving at all. No change takes place in our life in spite of all our yoga practice because we have not faced these fundamental questions.

In that great scripture, the Yoga Vasistha, there is a profound statement: "The mind alone is the cause of bondage and liberation." Why is it so? Is there bondage other than the thought that there is bondage? Is there a thing called attachment other than the thought? Where is this attachment? We must come face to face with it in order to see if it is attachment, or where the attachment is, otherwise we are merely fighting a shadow and as we are fighting it, the shadow becomes real. Liberation is possible only if we are able to come to grips with this fundamental question—where does this idea come from?

All these ideas arise in the mind. They are the activity of the ego or the self which thinks that 'I must somehow be superior to all other people.' 'I must be the only enlightened person.' Why don't we say: "God please let all men be enlightened."? Why do we demand 'me first'—in business, in politics or in spiritual politics? Because we have never bothered to look at this me, we have never bothered to grapple with this mind.

Analysing the mind is totally useless for two reasons: first and foremost, who is the analyser? Another thought, another idea, another facet of the mind. Is that facet capable of analysing the mind, the self or world? Secondly, the mind (or the 'me') is perhaps nothing more than an abbreviation of the word 'memory'. Is there a state where there is no me? What does it look like? The contents of this me, the stuff of which the mind is made, is something we don't know about without that which is known or that which enquires. This substance of the mind is also the mind, another idea. All these are ideas. Only when you come to this point where you see that everything and everywhere around is a trap, do you experience anguish: "Oh my God, where am I?" When one comes to that point there is a tremendous inner awakening, inner light, insight, wisdom—call it what you like—and one realises that objects exist only by courtesy of the mind.

Vichara is the awareness or the observation which is constantly looking for the arising of the idea called 'me', 'the self'. In the deep-sleep state the self and the world are absent. When sleep comes to an end, 'I am' arises—'I' become aware of what is called myself—and on the other end of the 'I am' thought is 'you', the world. The self is just an idea because it does not exist in one way or the other. This is illustrated beautifully in the Yoga Vasistha as also in the Mandukya Upanishad. The 'I', the ego or the self, is considered to be illusory, because when you begin to enquire into its nature, its substance, it is not found.

The 'I' does not exist, so what do 'I' do? Keep on looking. A great Indian saint, Ramana Maharshi, when he was a young boy, one day felt: "I am dying. I am dead." As he felt this, the heart stopped, the pulse stopped, circulation stopped, everything stopped—the body was getting blue. "But if I am dead, who sees I am dead, who says I am dead?"...In a moment of grace he attained enlightenment. He went to live in an underground cave pursuing this enquiry, and it is said that while he was engaged in this he would not even eat. When he was sitting in the cave people were pelting him with stones. The stones hit, there was pain. "Who is experiencing this pain?" "I." "Who am I?" When little insects crawled on his legs and thighs eating them away he was still saying: "Whose thigh is being eaten now? By whom?" If we can do that, we are practicing enquiry, *vichara*.

This enquiry must go right through, intensely, whatever happens, till there is dissolution of the idea of the self. Then the enquiry is meaningful, otherwise it is dangerous, leading to self-deception and deception of others. When there is this intensity, we can also practice *vichara* while sipping lovely coffee. "Who enjoys the flavour of this coffee?" That is *vichara*.

To remain in this state of awareness at least twenty-four hours of the day is *vichara*. It is very beautifully illustrated in the Buddha's sermon of the cobra in the room mentioned earlier. The state of mind in which you find yourself in that context is *vichara*. You are in meditation because at that moment everything is cobra, cobra, cobra! How does that concentration happen? You realise that unless you are totally vigilant, you will be finished. If you can live like this in the world, you realise that the self has been pushed away. *Hatha, Karma, Raja*, and *Bhakti Yoga* exist on the fundamental premise that the self is pushed out of the way—otherwise it will continue to create diversity and inner conflict.

Is it possible to live with this awareness which is constantly observing, till all trace of self is gone? When the self has been completely eradicated, who knows it? That is a very difficult problem. Therefore, there is no end to this enquiry. Once you are in it, you are in it for life. From there on there is no problem whatsoever. If there is some anxiety about life, enquire: "Whose life is it, and what does it matter?" Anxiety is a thought, an idea. Trace it, trace everything to its origin. Except for this tremendous vigilance or alertness which is constant, there is no other problem with *vichara*—no weakness, headache, sorrow or un-happiness because it is like fire that keeps burning, burning as long as there is the least bit of fuel. To this *vichara* everything is fuel.

The question arises: "In the meantime what do I do? I don't have this intensity or zeal and yet these ideas appeal to me." In the mean-time this *vichara* might form the ground of all that we do—whether it is spiritual practice, service of others or just words. *Vichara* may also be called the ground of all the experiences, whether they are pleasure or pain, happiness or unhappiness, praise or censure, honour or dis-honour. What is meant is that the moment there is an impact, let this *vichara* be set in motion. The moment we are hurt, ask: "What is hurt? Who is hurt? Why am I hurt?" That is possible for all of us.

Whatever course life takes, what it brings us and even how we react, may be beyond our control, but one thing is possible and that is that throughout our life, every day, every moment, this light of obser-vation can be kept bright. Never let it become dim. This is insisted upon by the Master. This light of observation is able to take care of the motivations. If they are wrong, they will disappear. If they are right, they are seen, they are observed and then transcended. And so throughout Vasistha says: "Keep this observation, this *vichara*, active and bright."

Vichara not only means enquiry and observation, but also deep contemplation of the truth, undeflected by the rational mind's activity of doubt, hope and despair. When the rational mind gives some expla-nation, the explanation is rejected as the product of the rational mind which is itself a product of ignorance. Who is interested in its answers? What is wanted is the truth!

Vichara is a dynamic and vital process. It is not something which is a dull routine or a habit pattern. The very essence of *vichara* is vitality: it must be alive. For this very reason the whole scripture looks at the same truth from as many different points of view as possible. 'What is this world? The world may be nothing more than an atom in existence'...'What is this world? Maybe it is nothing more than a dream'...One looks at this life and the world from as many points of view as possible so that all the assumed theories and realities get a good beating. Nothing is assumed, and if an assumption arises, you knock it down with something else. The road-block must be cleared so that the vision becomes undimmed. Wherever an assumption presents itself look into it from different angles and see if the truth concerning this can be sustained. That way the Master comes to the inescapable conclusion that the only thing that can really be affirmed concerning this life and concerning the entire creation is that the whole thing is pervaded by consciousness. That is the only thing that can be really real. All the rest is an assumption.

To sum up, *vichara* is movement of awareness in a very efficient way to trace the source of the arising of thoughts, emotions, feelings and, eventually, the very arising of the experiencer. The qualities of *sama*, when the mind stands controlled, as also *vichara*, are the antithesis of the arising of the experiencer and the perpetuation of this experiencer.

Constant and continuing *vichara* provides the right spirit to all our sacred and secular activities. A very beautiful example is given in the book called Ramayana. In it there is a sage called Hanuman, who was responsible for the victory of Rama, the hero of the epic. At the end of Hanuman's exploits, Rama asks him: "What do you think of our relationship? Who am I to you?" (That is very much like Jesus asking his disciples: "Who do you think I am?") The beautiful answer attributed to Hanuman is: "When I think I am the body, I am nothing but your servant. When I am doing some worship or when I am in a contemplative or mystic mood, I see you as the Lord and I am the *jiva* (living soul), part of you. When even that is transcended, even the idea of the self or the soul drops away, I am you, you are I, there is no distinction."

The Word Becomes Flesh

As long as the process called *sama*—control of mind and the process called *vichara*—direct observation of the source of these thoughts and feelings goes on without you, you will eventually see that naturally there is a certain type of contentment which is supremely blissful. You do not have to sit bolt upright in a meditative posture all the time: you may be doing whatever job is allotted to you in this world. You may be enjoying life, you may be suffering, but, whatever you may be doing, since the mind, the feelings, the thoughts are turned on their own source, as it were, there is contentment of a blissful nature. There is joyous participation in life while some restless hankering, craving or driving ambition that was previously there has come to an end. You feel hungry, eat; you feel tired, sleep; you want to get married and raise a family, do so. But all the time there is a supreme, blissful contentment without any driving ambition or craving. This is *santosha*, the third sentinel at the gateway of enlightenment.

Santosha is the total absence of craving. Do, do, do what has to be done but beware of craving. Can you engage yourself in all sorts of activities in the world, in life, without being motivated by cravings? As long as the self is there it will crave for one thing or the other, and as long as there is craving, one remains in delusion. Vasistha even says: "If somebody says: 'I am an enlightened man', observe him. An enlightened man does not have cravings."

In French, the word 'content' means 'happy'. So contentment, *santosha*, is a state of happiness. This can really and truly be experienced only if we change the meaning of that word completely. Contentment—what does the mind contain? That is the contentment. What is the content of desire, what is the content of all these emotions? As we go on this path we probably see that it is the mind that already contains all these. If it does not contain the experience of pleasure, we cannot experience pleasure. If it does not contain the experience of joy, we cannot experience joy. When that is realised then there is true contentment. Then there is no more craving or pursuit of pleasure. We are happy in whatever circumstances we are placed.

The master, Vasistha, also suggests that *vichara* or direct observation is better conducted with the aid of a teacher and a scripture. (The scripture may be a text that the teacher might select or the teacher's own words.) Why is this suggested? For a very simple reason: it is possible for us to feel highly competent to conduct this *vichara* on our own but we may be tempted to allow the mind to run off at a tangent. We may not know how to direct this attention in an intelligent way. We may not know what correct understanding of the truth means. We might mistake the chaff for the wheat. It is the master who says: "No! Push a little more."

The last sentinel is this *sadhusangama* or *satsanga*. *Satsanga* is used as an adjective without a noun: keeping company with the good. That is precisely what it is. But what kind of good? *Sadhusangama* includes the people, the scriptures, thoughts, food, feelings, everything. Seek the company of good, holy men, if you can find them. If you are holy and you are looking for someone holy you will find plenty of holy men and women in this world. If you are vicious and if you are looking for some vicious company you will find everybody vicious. It depends entirely upon you. If you find some holy people resort to their company. If you do not find them resort to their teachings, the holy books and scriptures.

Also ensure that your thoughts and feelings are honest and good, so that the mind, the senses and the intelligence are constantly being fed with something healthy and edifying and inner violent reactions are avoided. The inner reactions cannot be totally stopped, for as long as one is alive one is going to react; as long as one is alive the mind is going to function through some kind of feeling or thought. If these are within manageable proportions some stimulation might be helpful, but if they are beyond your control all the time, then tremendous inner tension must result and you will battle. That which does not excite you beyond endurance is good. Life is not dull at all if one appreciates the movement but as it comes along, see that there is no violent excitement or reaction.

We are not asked to resort to good company and avoid evil company in order to empower us to judge the people or the things around us, but in order to caution that we should be extremely vigilant and avoid those influences that are a distraction from this extremely delicate adventure of *vichara*. Anything that distracts us from this is to be avoided.

Vasistha again and again points out that we are not here to judge the world. If we were given that privilege, we would most likely have the biggest ego in the world. There is no judgment involved in words like good and bad, but these words have to be used merely as a form of instruction—please do not take them as absolute truths. It is quite simple: "This is company which is unsuitable to me at this point: it distracts the mind and the attention from pursuing this extremely delicate *vichara*. And here is company which is favourable to *vichara*." In this there is not judgment or condemnation. I resort to the favourable company and I keep away from unfavourable company. As a matter of fact. what may be unwise or undesirable company for one may be the ideal company for somebody else also pursuing the spiritual path. Hence there are so many ashrams in India, so many gurus and so many diametrically opposed practices. If one path does not suit you leave it alone and go somewhere else. So, *satsanga, sadhusangama,* means: that company which is favourable to you in your search for the ultimate truth, and in this extremely delicate adventure of *vichara*.

Whatever be the condition in which our whole being flows towards the truth and not away from it, that is *satsanga*. It may be the morning newspaper! In it we see all the horrors that are going on and suddenly we feel: "Oh my God, I do not want this world again." Swami Sivananda once said: "I must suffer intensely before I die." He said that that suffering must be so intense that the very roots of desire to live again should be uprooted. That is a strong commandment.

The scriptures or holy men stimulate the mind and the intellect in the right direction. They question our scale of values. They ask inconvenient questions, and that is the starting point for *vichara*. We have allowed the mind, the attention, to drift where it will. We have allowed the mind to become aware of something external. But we have not allowed the attention, the observation, to look at the mind itself and ask some fundamental questions. It is possible that during this *satsanga* or study of the scriptures some such questions arise. "I have taken for granted that my happiness comes from something which I acquire or possess or seek. Is it real? Why do I pursue an object? What happens if I discover that the object itself does not exist except as a projection of my own mind?" That is what is suggested in the scripture or in the satsanga. And as we continue this *vichara*, we begin to observe some vital phenomena that had been taken for granted.

When we expose the mind and heart to *satsanga* in this manner, a subtle revolution takes place within us of which we are often unaware. When we participate in some exercise class we become aware that the waistline goes down, aches and pains disappear...the change is measurable. But it is not possible to measure the change produced by *satsanga*. Yet this change is so great, so profound, so marvellous, that suddenly people around you feel that there has been a change.

Sometimes it is best that one does not notice this change. All growth is subtle and imperceptible. Growth which you can demonstrably notice is usually dangerous. It is: good, better, worst (the grammar changes here). Suppose a young man stopped the smoking habit after he came into contact with some spiritual teacher. That is good—he becomes good. Then, under the instruction of his teacher, he grows more and more in goodness—which means that after some time he becomes better. Now, because he does not smoke or drink or go to movies or eat meat, he <u>feels</u> that he has become much better. At this moment he starts criticising others. He becomes so arrogant, so conceited, that he really becomes worst: worse than he ever was! So, growth that can be exhibited is cancerous and he who wants to demonstrate such spiritual growth becomes what the first five letters of the word 'demonstrate' spell. He becomes a demon.

True spiritual growth is continuous, extremely subtle and, one can say, unending. My guru often emphasised that the spiritual aspirant must be vigilant to the end. He used a Tamil expression which meant, 'Till the end of your physical existence, be careful; there is within you the potential of evil'. You are good now, you are better than what you were some time ago, but as long as the embodiment lasts, as long as the mind is associated with the body and, through the body with the world, there is the possibility of evil rising again. So be careful till the end.

If these few facts are kept in mind there is no chance for the conceited arrogance to rise in you. You vigilantly observe more of your own inner weaknesses than of whatever good may be in you. You may feel that you are becoming better but at the same time you realise that there is still a lot of dirt within you. You know that most of your house is clean but there are some parts that have still to be cleaned. This dual realisation is the purpose of *satsanga*. Gradually seeping through, the truth gets assimilated and thus the word becomes flesh.

Shankaracharya, one of the great masters of more recent times, describes very simply what *satsanga* amounts to. "*Satsanga* must lead to *nihsanga*." *Nihsanga* means: one is not keen on any company at all. If this *satsanga* does not lead one to a certain psychological isolation, psychological distance, then that is not such good company, however noble it may look from the outside. *Satsanga* is that which enables us to live in a certain type of isolation, without attachment. We do not feel lonely but we enjoy being alone. We are not antisocial, but we enjoy our own company. This is the state where we can investigate the truth concerning the mind and its source without being distracted by other influences. It is then that we discover for ourselves that whether or not there are provoking external circumstances, thoughts and feelings arise. Suddenly we realise that the previous habit of blaming all these on external forces was nonsense. And there we begin to study ourselves.

A restless mind is its own worst enemy. This understanding arises when, through *satsanga*, one gets into the state of what I would call spiritual isolation. This is a necessary step to the realisation of cosmic oneness. In this spiritual isolation all the deluded ideas that were previously entertained come to an end. And when such delusion has disappeared, or as it gets weakened, there is a steady understanding of the truth concerning the mind the self and its activities. Then we attain freedom here and now: freedom from delusion, freedom from illusion, freedom from restlessness, freedom from craving, freedom from pursuit of pleasure and therefore freedom from sorrow.

In Search of Mind

Without the discovery of the source of the mind control is impossible. We can juggle on and play with all sorts of things. We can even develop extraordinary psychic powers—ESP, ABC, XYZ!—but without a correct understanding of the source of mind or the very nature of the stuff of which the mind, thought, feeling is made, no control is possible. It is like trying to drive a car while lying in bed—it is not possible. One must get into the car and know how to handle it. *Vichara* or direct observation enables us to discover the stuff of which the mind is made.

When we apply this *vichara* to the source of the mind, to the source of thought, to the source of feelings, what do we discover? We discover some sort of an intelligence and we discover that there is a movement, a flow of energy. When that flow of energy is not there, there is sleep. When the energy begins to vibrate a bit, we dream and then we wake up. There is intelligence but, if we are observing very intensely and carefully, there also seem to be some grooves in that intelligence through which this energy seems to flow more freely.

This is no great discovery of a tremendous truth: in psychology it is called the law of association. Vaguely it could be the law of association of thoughts, association of ideas. Hence Vasistha tells us: "This tree called the mind has grown out of two seeds. One is called *prana spanda*—movement of *prana*, movement of life-force, vitality, and the other is *vasana*. What is *vasana*? It is something like a dress, a covering. It is something that makes a thing appear as if it has a form—like the shape and the rubber of the balloon. It is the source of all names and forms. *Vasana* is that impulse within that appears in front of us as an object. If the *vasana* was absent we would experience this world as God sees it. It is the *vasana* that generates the idea that this is a man. An ant would not call this a young man ... to the ant this is a mountain. The ant's *vasana* is different. If a hungry tiger happens to come, it would not call this a young man, but breakfast or lunch or supper! ... because that is its *vasana*.

All our experiences and expressions leave some traces on this intelligence and these, by repeatedly being re-expressed and re-experienced, cut grooves. At one stage the grooves are called *samskaras* and at another stage they are called *vasanas*. All sorts of words and expressions have been used to translate *vasanas*—tendency, mental conditioning, habit pattern—but I do not think any one of these is really adequate. *Vasana* is a sort of mental conditioning, a psychological predisposition: the grooves have been cut so that when the energy moves, it flows along these grooves and a restlessness is created in the intelligence. That restlessness is called mind. Hence, at one point Vasistha declares that mind and restlessness are synonyms.

When we bear this in mind, a shocking truth emerges: if we are able to control and still the mind, there is no mind. It is possible that such a state exists but we cannot bring it about. A mind that is totally free of restlessness is like dehydrated water. If such a thing does not exist then mind also does not exist without restlessness. Hence Vasistha, while he treats of the no-mind state, calls it *sattva*. *Sattva* is the radiance of the reality which is way beyond the mind. When the mind has ceased to be mind, when all restlessness has ceased, mind is no-mind—it becomes *sattva*. You are that. Or, not <u>you</u> are that, <u>that</u> is that. God realises himself.

This whole thing called mind is nothing but a vibration—*prana spanda*—the movement of *prana*. In this intelligence, mysteriously, past expressions and experiences have left a mark and therefore a little channel has been cut. Energy passes along those channels again and again, bringing up the same patterns of thought, desires, cravings, feelings and so on. The mind starts flowing in one direction and then suddenly a memory is awakened ... the mind starts flowing in another direction. But one thing is unmistakable and that is that there is a thought and habit pattern. And one person's thought pattern is very different from another's thought pattern.

All of us are subject to habit patterns. If we observe very carefully, the mind loves habit. Strangely enough there is a tremendously beautiful lesson for us in the mind's habit of forming habits and functioning along those habit patterns. Why does the mind create and flow along these habit patterns? If we watch very carefully we will realise that it is to conserve energy. This is one of the greatest secrets that is built into us.

When you were learning to drive a car, do you remember how you used to struggle to coordinate the clutch release and the shift? It was not so easy! But now you do it while talking or listening to the radio! Why? It has become habit. You do not think about it at all. Your hands and legs function as if they are the extensions of the car. Energy is conserved when there is a smooth, undisturbed, undistracted flow of awareness. That is the function of habit. Once it becomes a habit, the energy flows without distraction, without dissipation and therefore there seems to be no loss of energy. Incidentally, that is what is called *brahmacharya* (traditionally translated as celibacy): the total energy and total consciousness flows unidirectionally is is not distracted and dissipated here and there.

In practice, these *vasanas* amount to patterns of behaviour and thought which have become habits. It is extremely important to understand them clearly, yet *vasana* is also extremely difficult to understand. Hence even such an iconoclastic scripture as the Yoga Vasistha seems to compromise a little in order to divide this indivisible awareness into what psychology might call ego and the superego. Vasistha seems to suggest that *vasana* can be pure and impure, just like a coating on the mirror or tinted glasses. Some glasses improve the vision, some tint it, while some others disturb or hamper it. So Vasistha seems to suggest that there are different types of *vasanas*: one that tends toward enlightenment and the other that seems to veil it even more strongly. It is possible for one to strengthen the good habits and weaken the bad habits. If, in associating with the sages, one is able to expose the brighter side of one's nature, one's better nature, and thus strengthen it, the darker side is weakened. When this psychological tendency or habit pattern is healthy, spiritual, holy, it becomes, according to Vasistha, again, an adorable conditioning.

For practical purposes and for the time being we accept that there may be a division between good and bad habits. But both are habits and as long as they are habits they are destructive, they are obstructive of self-knowledge. However, a good habit may be less obstructive than a bad habit. Drinking a glass of orange juice every morning is a habit, drinking a cup of coffee every morning is a habit, but one is supposed to be good and the other is supposed to be bad. In the same way an ordinary person might be arrested by the police and put into iron chains while some holy or respectable person may also be arrested and put into some kind of a gold bracelet. Both are shackles (but I suppose there is some difference between the two!).

When we decide that these *vasanas* are getting heavier we might want to change them. Behaviour is a heavy expression of our being: when our being becomes heavier, an action arises (behaviour). When this becomes even more heavy we become a burden on earth and at that point we might feel like changing the pattern of behaviour. Be very careful here: we are merely changing the pattern of behaviour. The grooves are still being cut, but we hope they do not lead to unhealthy or unholy behaviour.

What happens to the previous bad *vasana* now that we are cultivating good thought patterns, good habit patterns? When we change these habit patterns, physical or mental, having decided that the previous lot was unholy—that is, suddenly we change to orange juice instead of drinking coffee in the morning—have we got rid of the previous habit patterns which were considered impure? No! We have merely superimposed upon them a new habit pattern. We have masked them so that as the outer 'perfume' begins to wear out, the original habits become stronger and stronger and stronger!

In one part of India the word *vasana* also means 'smell'. It has a rather interesting connotation: if you handle some incense or garlic and you want to wipe your hands clean, the smell is still there. All right, wash your hands . . . the smell is still there. Even if you wash with perfumed soap and water, the smell is so strong that you can smell the soap and the garlic. That is *vasana*: the mental conditioning has been implanted so nicely that whatever you do the 'smell' still comes out.

If our behaviour is good, society is highly pleased. But if we wear perfume to mask some bad odour, that does not solve the problem. Cosmetic treatment, especially of psychological, spiritual and moral problems, is worse than nuisance. It can be quite deceptive and therefore destructive. This is the danger of dealing with these *vasanas*. We have to understand them very thoroughly and clearly; and the understanding, if it is properly undertaken, is absolutely easy.

Thus the great sage Vasistha, after having declared assertively that nobody can enlighten you, nobody can free you from the bondage that only you feel, concedes emphatically that this *vichara* can be and preferably should be done in the company of a teacher and, perhaps, with the aid of a scripture. Why? Because we may think that the old habit patterns or habit moulds are being broken and new, healthy, holy habits are being formed, but it may not be so. It is extremely difficult for one to be one's own judge. Therefore, resort to good company, the company of an enlightened one or a more advanced student—someone who is like a monitor, who might be able to suggest that this is not what you are or what you want to do. It is not easy to know for oneself what these *vasanas* are and how they obstruct, distract and disturb the vision of truth. But with the help of an enlightened teacher it is extremely easy to deal with them. Understanding the dynamics of the *vasanas* instantly frees one from them.

Great masters who have adopted the practice of *vichara* in preference to all other forms of spiritual practice have recommended *pranayama* (breath control) as something useful for dealing with the *vasanas*. We are not asked to stop the movement of *prana*. When *pranayama* is practiced it brings about a certain stillness in the movement of energy which in turn reflects on the mind so that a certain tranquility is experienced which facilitates *vichara* which facilitates the direct looking into of the source of the mind, thoughts and feelings.

If it is possible to sustain this *vichara* constantly it is not at all difficult to realise that in the intelligence there is a movement of this energy along certain paths, creating certain patterns. This is the mind. But there is nobody to claim ownership of this mind. In our practice of meditation it is possible to see that this body as well as the source of these feelings, the source of these thoughts, belong to some other agency, not 'me'. That truth can be easily realised if one is constantly vigilant. It needs constant vigilance because one moment of unawareness installs the 'me' on the pedestal as an unquestionable reality and the whole game is lost.

The moment the dissociation of 'mind' and 'me' has been achieved there is a tremendous control of the mind. The foolish idea that 'this is my mind' has been diffused, abandoned and when this happens, mineness is gone. There is life, of course, life goes on. There is tremendous intelligence and that intelligence guides life in its own way and, as we would say: "God's will is done."

[107]

A Matter of Identification

In the Yoga Vasistha and in some other scriptures like the Bhagavatam there is a lovely saying: "You fool, why do you think that that body is yours? There are so many claimants! While that body is alive, your employer claims that it belongs to him, that it must serve him; your wife claims that it belongs to her; your children claim it belongs to them. And when that body stops breathing, a vulture claims that it belongs to it; the worms of the earth claim it belongs to them; and fire and air think it belongs to them!" This body itself belongs to heaven knows what but it does not belong to a thing called 'me'. It is the 'me' that says: "This body is 'me'" or "It belongs to 'me'". That creates confusion, otherwise life goes on smoothly.

The body is subject to hunger, thirst, sleep, fatigue and so many other things. These are inherent in it, beyond the 'me'. They are not within the reach of the ego. What a beautiful setup this is! There is consciousness or awareness in the body not because of any extraordinary qualification on 'my' part, but only because there is consciousness or intelligence everywhere—omnipresent! And there is energy in this body because there is energy, there is *prana*, everywhere. It is that energy that creates what is called hunger and what is called thirst. That message is carried by the same intellect to God knows where and food is produced.

What is needed by this body is produced somewhere. You can see this most dramatically between the mother and infant. The infant needs milk and the mother's breast produces that milk. Fantastic! The mother does not produce the milk, it is there! The need of the infant is experienced by this combination of energy and intelligence and because neither that energy nor that intelligence is confined to the infant's little body but are omnipresent: the message gets through. This is the fact of cosmic intelligence.

In that cosmic intelligence, cut by billions of grooves, there are waves and waves of energy floating around everywhere. One spark of awareness which arises somewhere identifies itself with a certain bunch of grooves and from there on these become 'my' experiences, 'my' behaviour and 'my' action. Only that which says: 'This is my thought', 'This is my action', links or tunes itself to those grooves and the habit or *vasana* is born. It is very much like radio waves. We cannot hear them but the radio can. Only that which is tuned to them will receive them. Consciousness or intelligence is indivisible—one indistinguishable mass of energy vibrations. Yet something identifies itself with this body and not with another. Something says: "This is 'I', 'you', 'he'." This is the most tragic fact and from there starts all the mischief. How does this happen? We do not know... but that identification is not the truth. It is a mere matter of identification.

We can see this tragically and traumatically in the case of people or things with which we establish some relationship. I consider a person to be my great friend, my very dear friend—an identification. If a total stranger insults 'my dearest friend' I get hurt and want to break his neck! I rationalise this saying: "My friend has been insulted so I must stand up and fight for him." Is this friend so weak and incapable of defending himself? We call it sentimentalism, loyalty, all sorts of strange words, but the simplest act is that it is utter foolishness and stupidity. We must first look into this a bit more carefully and realise that rationalisation is self-deception and a confession of stupidity.

To the extent I think these are 'my' experiences I am bound to experience those experiences... like dream. Sleeping in the same bed, two people have completely different experiences. We dismiss those experiences saying: "It is only dream." But these experiences are also dream! And to the extent that we identify ourselves with these habit patterns floating everywhere we will experience happiness or unhappiness. There is a story in the Yoga Vasistha to illustrate this:

A holy man prayed to God: "God, I would like to experience

your *maya*. *Maya* is the illusory power of God—the power of illusion of the divine. Swami Sivananda described *maya* as follows: *maya* is not something which you can avoid, push away; it cannot be defined properly. That which makes you forget the truth that you have glimpsed is *maya*.

God replied: "Okay."

After a few weeks this holy man one day plunged into the river for his bath and ablutions. Suddenly he collapsed and died and his body was cremated.

Five hundred years later he came alive as a fœtus in some woman in the Central African jungle. After lots of trouble he was born, screaming. He endured the filthy atmosphere, the mosquitoes and flies—a miserable life. He grew up, married a terrible-looking woman and they had more terrible-looking children. Then there was famine in the country and many people left. He also went away.

As he was wandering he happened to pass through a small town where he saw an elephant rushing towards him. He stood petrified. The elephant had a garland in its trunk which it dropped around his neck. Then there was a celebration. Why? The previous king had died without an heir to the throne so the elders of the place had appointed this elephant to choose the next king. And the elephant had chosen this man! He was put on the elephant, everybody danced and he was taken to the palace and put on the throne.

He was only a tribesman with no idea of what either a king or a government meant. But once you sit on a seat you function—the seat makes you function. Within three days you find out how everything works!

So he ruled the kingdom very nicely.

One day a group of musicians, tribesmen, was singing outside the palace. The king walked out unaccompanied by his retinue and not heavily adorned. One of the tribesmen recognised him as one of their tribe and called him by his original name. He was embarrassed and tried to make a retreat but the palace servants and ministers had already heard this. They said: "Is he such an untouchable tribesman? He has been our king for so long and we have knelt before him and greeted him! We have been serving a devil so far. What should we do?" They called the Brahmins who said: "There is no expiation for this sin. We must all commit suicide." So they raised a huge bonfire and one by one they jumped in. When the king heard of this holocaust he thought: "It is on account of me that all these people died. Let me also jump." And so he jumped . . .

> Suddenly the holy man was still standing in the water. He had plunged under the water for only three or four seconds and within those few seconds all this drama had taken place! He thought: "I asked God to show me His illusory power. I think this silly drama was it."

But while this drama was in progress it was hundreds of years in heaven or hell, then nine months in somebody's body, growing up, ruling as king and so on! We experience this every night in dream. The dream might have lasted for fifteen or twenty seconds but we live a whole lifetime in that dream.

When he came out of the water he realised that the places he had dreamt of were real places. So he went to those places and verified that these events had in fact taken place!

Now Rama asks the question: "How was it possible for one's own hallucination to be factually verified in what is the real world?" Listen very carefully, this is a tricky thing which may take ten years to understand clearly. Here the scripture says: "It is possible because occasionally your consciousness identifies itself with something that happened somewhere else." This teaching instantly blows to pieces our conception of a soul as a sort of solid reality. Coming back to this thing called dream. Is the dreamer myself or not? Who else? Yet it does not seem to be so because in dream I often dream of things which I would never dream of dreaming at other times! Maybe the window was open and some energy vibration (or *vasana*) which was floating around happened to pass through my head.

Once we get into this teaching we suddenly think anything is possible. But not necessarily to 'me'. There is no 'me'. "Me' is merely a bit of memory. It is just one thought, one spark of awareness which, for unknown reasons, identifies itself with a certain body and a certain pattern of behaviour. Why does it identify itself with this body? There is absolutely no rational explanation. When this fact is directly seen three things will take place simultaneously: the habit mould immediately gets blown into a million fragments; I am not tuned to any energy patterns that may be floating around and therefore I am not bothered; and since there is no tuning in, there is peace.

What are our prejudices and our biases made of? Are they real? What is the pleasure-sensation made of? It is just a sensation, a neurological response. If you kiss the left cheek and smack the right cheek, probably the response of each cheek is the same. The left cheek was excited because it was kissed and the right cheek was excited because it was slapped. The excitement could have been almost identical but what is the difference? The difference is merely a matter of convention. When the intelligence sees this there is enlightenment.

That intelligence which sees these two sensations as identical knows how to take the appropriate action. When the sameness of the substance of all the experiences of pleasure, pain, honour, dishonour, success, failure, happiness, unhappiness, friend, enemy, love, hate and so on is realised by this inner intelligence then we are no longer enslaved, governed or controlled by our tendencies, mental impressions and psychological conditioning. We may still respond to pleasure and to pain in a certain way but the mind and the memory are not involved. It would not do to bring the mind in here, again to form another concept of identity. The inner intelligence must be awake to see this. Then a very different vision arises.

That vision also sees the world in a different light. The tendencies, mental impressions or psychological conditioning cease to interfere in life, in action, in relationships and do not determine our experience or our expression. The experience or the expression goes on, determined by the reality or the truth (this is one of the characteristics of enlightenment) and therefore there are no cravings and no hate because these are assumed realities, assumed concepts.

What is mind? Mind is merely that which identifies itself with the habit mould. When the identification is broken, shattered, mind is no mind, mind is gone. Then this supreme intelligence remains as intelligence. In that intelligence there is really no *vasana*. There are no grooves. It is part of the whole cosmos. Just as wave is a wave only in relation to something which is not the wave, us; *vasana* as *vasana* is *vasana* only in relation to us—to a stupid mind. What is the content of a wave? Water, sea. There is no need to call it a wave. The ocean does not call it a wave, it is ocean—water. What is the content of the *vasana*? The same consciousness that is everywhere—one indivisible consciousness. Immediately that becomes clear the mind ceases to be mind. The mind becomes no mind and the truth is directly perceived and realised.

Life goes on blissfully, peacefully, in an enlightened way. Such an enlightened life cannot be predetermined because it is beyond logic. That is what we call divine will. In such a state you will be exactly what God made you to be, as simple as that. Divine will means 'not my will' but whatever has to be is. That involves and implies total surrender of the ego, total cessation of the ego-sense. When the light of truth arises the shadow of ignorance and its offspring called the ego ceases to exist and life is blissful, peaceful and divine.

The Marionettes' Game

The root cause of the restlessness of the mind is that every present situation is a challenge to which one little image in our consciousness responds. As one image responds the others feel threatened and also jump up. Then there is confusion. I like somebody and want to go forward and hug him but something pushes me, something inhibits me, something frightens me, something threatens me and so on. Each situation is played entirely by these marionettes. Therefore there is this seemingly unending restlessness of the mind and this restlessness is the mind. This mental restlessness is also called by the name *vasana*. The two do not make a cause-and-effect sequence but they are two sides of the same coin. If you knock the one down the other is gone.

Vasana is a lovely word used innumerable times in the scripture but is almost impossible to translate. However, it has been translated into 'psychological tendency', 'psychological predisposition'. What do these mean? We use all these lovely words without understanding anything about them. Psychological predisposition simply means one of these marionettes jumping up. 'I am predisposed to do this' simply means that there is no 'me' at all because all these marionettes put together is what I call my personality or 'me'. So it is not, as it were, a psychological predisposition in me, it is me. If I knock off all these images, one after the other, there is no 'me' left. Whatever makes you act or react as you do—that is called *vasana*.

Desire, craving, fear, anxiety are unrelated to life, except that they complicate life. This does not mean that if we were totally rid of cravings, fear and anxiety life would become static; nor does it mean that we make things happen by craving, fear or anxiety. Let us take a simple example: it is winter and it is dark at about five o'clock in the morning. You are excitedly telling everyone around you: "Oh, I wish the sun would rise, it would be glorious." You can repeat this sentence like a mantra two hundred times but the sun will not rise. But watch: you are excitedly expecting the sun to rise and when it does rise you say: "Aha, here it is!" The sun rose totally unmindful of your excitement but since you were excitedly anticipating that event the event made you even more excited. The excitement with which you anticipated that event is carried over as the excitement you experience and the mind relates to that event. You may be excited, you may not be excited, the sun will still rise. If you were excited the excitement would continue after the sun rose. If you were not excited but calm that calmness would continue after the sun rose.

The same thing happens at night. Some people are afraid of the dark. But whether they are afraid that the sun is going to set or whether they are happy the sun is still going to set. The setting of the sun has nothing to do with private whims and fancies but because these people work themselves up into this anxiety, when the sun sets, they collapse. Whatever happens in this world, whatever happens in life, will continue to happen and nothing will stop it.

Into this dream of life we introduce all our fancies, fantasies and neuroses. Then, having introduced these fancies, we experience them as if they were somehow related to us so that even the arising or the cessation of an event was dependent upon our promptings. But it has nothing at all to do with us or our fears. One who realises that sees that life or the events in this world are totally unrelated to his cravings, desires or otherwise.

The cravings will only affect me. They are not related at all to what is happening. My wish or my fear do not materialise. They materialise only as my own experiences, later. Life goes on totally unmindful of my private reactions. When I understand that it is not my excitement that pushes this situation up nor my fear that pushes that situation down I am able to observe what happens within me without complicating it with external phenomena. You may have a gun hanging from your belt and I may be afraid, but as long as I relate my fear to that, I am not able to observe that fear. For instance, if you were my bodyguard I would be quite happy to see that gun hanging from your belt! There-fore my fear is totally unrelated to the external event. When I see that then I am able to observe what goes on within me and I see that these are merely some of the marionettes reacting. This is the beauty of *vichara* or observation.

Related to this is the whole concept of creation and dissolution. How do all these come into being and how do they dissolve? You are already aware of the fundamental philosophical concept where it is held that whatever is in the microcosm is in the macrocosm. Whatever applies to the individual applies to the cosmos, and whatever applies to the cosmos applies to the individual. The two are indistinguishably, indivisibly one. In the Yoga Vasistha it is beautiful to see that when it looks as though the author is talking about individual creation sud-denly he changes and makes it look as though he is talking about the cosmic creation, almost as if to say: "Why make a distinction?"

What is the process of involution and what is the process of evolu-tion? Or, what are the steps to ignorance of self-knowledge and what are the steps to enlightenment or self-knowledge? There is a very beautiful description and I will give you the steps. Then we will see how they can be applied to our life as a whole and even to our daily life and to the birth and dissolution of the cosmos. The material universe comes into being, exists for some time going through a lot of changes and is dissolved. You and I come into this world, we are born, we continue to live, thrive, decay and then disappear. The same thing applies to our daily life: every morning we are born, we grow and we decay—in the evening we are already stooping a little bit and instead of getting into the grave we get into bed! One is not fundamentally different from the other.

I am relating all this to our daily life so that we can see how very minutely the yogis have observed this daily life. The first state in the process of involution, called *bija jagrat*, is just before we really wake up but it is not always that we become aware of this state. *Bija* means seed and *jagrat* means wakefulness. I am in bed, asleep, then the sleep seems to come to an end and I am about to wake up. I feel the sheet and I feel the bed but it is not as though "I am sleeping in this bed"; nothing seems to be real, nothing seems to be unreal; there is not even a distinction between real and unreal. But this is not self-knowledge, this is not God-realisation, this is not floating in space because I am about to wake up. This means that all the mischief that I am capable of is in a seed state.

The next state is called *jagrat* or wakefulness and in that period I experience: "Ah, I am here and this is my bed." I am just waking up: "This is my house, I am sleeping in my house, I am sleeping in my room, this is me." The person who is waking up at this point is unaware of the whole world but is only aware of these two concepts: 'this is me', and 'this is my bed, this is my room, this is my house'.

The next state is *maha jagrat*; *maha* means great. This same wakefulness has expanded enormously and 'this is me' and 'this is mine' have also expanded. Instead of merely saying: "This is me", I have now woken up to the feeling that the 'me' is composed of a tremendous number of qualifications: 'I am a doctor', 'I am a yogi', 'I am this', 'I am that'—all these wake up. This is merely an expansion of the first wakefulness: the whole world has come into being.

Then comes a very subtle and beautiful state: 'this is me and this is the world'—relationship begins to appear in this consciousness. The Master calls it *jagrat svapna*; *jagrat* means waking and *svapna* means dream. All our wonderful relationships with all these diverse beings in the universe with which we connect ourselves within our own imagination are nothing more than a waking dream. You think 'you are', I think 'I am' and 'I' think 'you are' and so I imagine some kind of relationship with you. It is nothing more than a 'waking dream'. Since our whole life seems to be based only on this, the Master calls the entire life a long dream, nothing more than that. Only one thing is awake: the feeling 'I am' and that has projected innumerable objects with which it enters into certain relationships, all these being mere dreams.

The fundamental wakefulness of 'I am' is the only thing that seems to be real in this world-game. The rest is dream. We enter into these relationships and we think they are all real, factual, unshakeable, unquestionable, until we begin to question that. We have changed so often that we do not even realise when we are in the next dream. We do not realise: "I have walked into this illusion so often and I have been disillusioned so often. Why must I get into this again?" This does not occur to us because while we are engaged in that dream that dream seems to be real. This is the tragedy.

There is another aspect: while life goes on like this—'this is me, this is mine', 'he is my brother and she is my sister', 'this is my wife and that is my husband, father, mother, children, etc.'—to some extent these things seem to share some quality of truth. Why? Because they are all related to me and this 'me' seems to be a stable factor.

In the waking dream there is some mixture of reality and unreality but all of us are capable of the next, which is *svapna*, pure dream. This does not mean the dream in bed but our present dream. Having heard all this, we go and sit in the meditation room or at the beach and we begin: "Oh, it is marvellous, I am going to be enlightened one of these days and once I am enlightened, what a wonderful thing—one foot here and the other foot on Mars..." The whole thing is imagination and this kind of day-dreaming is called *svapna*. We think we are awake but we are not. We are completely disconnected from reality; it is some kind of hallucination, day-dreaming. That is also part of our daily life.

Then there is *svapna jagrata* which means *svapna*, dream, and *jagrata*, waking. Here again there is a mixture of something that is not and something that is. We revive the memory of a past experience as if it were happening now. We are all capable of this—pure and simple but vivid memory. If we were awake to wisdom even the past experience as it happened would have a different character—we would neither enjoy nor suffer with it. But we revive this memory now and experience it as if it were happening now. That is another state of mind we pass through every day. Finally, when we get tired to all this we go to sleep and forget everything. This is the story of a person's daily life.

This is the story of our total life-span. We are born—a little baby in whom all the seeds of potential mischief are lying dormant. Then the baby wakes up to the feeling: "I am So-and-so, this is my father, this is my mother." Later the baby grows a little more and its world seems to expand. Can you visualise this? As we grow up—three, four, five years old—our world seems to expand far beyond our house, to our neighbours, to our friends, to our school-mates. The world seems to grow· *maha jagrat*. Next we forge relationships which do not exist: 'He is my friend and he is my enemy; he is my rival and he is my competitor' and so on. We may throw out these relationships as dreams but they return to us as ropes, tying us to all sorts of difficult situations. Caught in this web woven by ourselves, we dream of liberation and freedom, we dream of pleasure and happiness. These are all nothing more than dreams.

Then we come to the stage where the only thing we are left with is memory. All the good things are past and we go into the woods and think of all the nice things that happened, experiencing them as if they were happening now! This goes on for some time and then we seem to get tired of all this experiencing and reviving of memories and hallucinations and we fall asleep and do not wake up. (We wake up in another body!) Thus what applies to our daily life also applies to the whole life-span.

It is also possible that the entire cosmos or universe (or what we call our solar system—the universe we are aware of) also passes through the same stages. In this little body there are billions of cells, each of them functioning in a dual relationship. That is, each cell seems to be independent of the other and yet all cells are interrelated. Each cell seems to know its function and performs only its function, seemingly independent of the others. It can even fight with other cells of one living being so that if that being dies all the cells die. Each cell seems to function independently up to a point but not totally.

Is it possible that even now all these hundreds and thousands of stars that we see in the night are similarly cells in one enormous body of a 'Mr. So-and-so' (it does not have to be 'God') and that we are all tiny little microscopic entities in that enormous body? It is quite possible. And all the things which we call creation, preservation and dissolution happen in that enormous body. Creation exists and so does dissolution. That cosmic being also undergoes these several stages of involution.

Worlds Within Worlds

Earlier on we were introduced to the three categories *chid akasa*, *chitta akasa* and *bhutakasa*. Let us reconsider them here. What is called space is characterised as something filled with intelligence. That is *chid akasa*. But though the entire universe is throbbing with consciousness, awareness, intelligence, in *chid akasa* there is no universe; it is just one mass of consciousness. How large is it? The question is absurd because there is no space in that consciousness. It is precisely like dream. When you dream of visiting America there is no America in your bedroom, no America can be accommodated in your brain but in dream it is there. Where?...Please don't try to understand this, it is impossible. I just wanted you to have a glimpse of this spaceless dimension known as consciousness.

In that vast, illimitable, inexpressible, indescribable plane of pure consciousness, thoughts, ideas, notions, dreams are floating around. Suddenly one of these ideas begins to form a molecule of thought, as it were: 'I'...'I am', and proceeds to function on that basis: 'I am seeing this', 'I am seeing that'—the 'that' becomes an object. That 'I am' is, merely for our understanding, described as *chitta akasa*—what you and I in our ignorance would designate as mind. All these float in what is called physical space, *bhutakasa*.

None of these is essentially real or, at least the latter two are not real at all. What is meant by physical space? Of late there are scientific volumes by the hundreds, bringing home to us the relativity of space, which means the non-absolute existence of space. For instance, we ask a very familiar question: "What happens to us after we die?" Where do we go and how long does it take for us to reincarnate? It is a very valuable question to find an answer to, especially if you are married and you want to meet your partner on the other side! But there is a big problem: the three fundamental factors which we accept unquestion-ingly—time, space and materiality or substantiality—are totally de-pendent on brain function.

It is one time in Johannesburg, some other time in San Francisco; it is one day here, some other day somewhere else. Time is a convenient tool that we have invented in order to come together—we are able to adjust our watches in such a way that we can all assemble at the correct time. This thing called time is built into the computer known as the brain.

In the same way, because the brain has been conditioned to mea-sure space in terms of vision, sight, it is baffled when it sees just space. It is very easy, if we are flying at a high altitude, to look out of the plane window and see no space at all. We have no idea how much distance we are able to see. What is meant by space? We used to take Swami Sivananda in a taxi to a place far away from the ashram so that he could walk on flat ground. On one such occasion there was a very majestic and tame elephant standing there. I wanted to take a picture that would look as though Swamiji was brushing shoulders with the elephant but Swamiji would not go too close to it. It is not difficult at all to take such a picture if you know how to handle a camera. The space can be eliminated by training the camera in such a way that the two shoulders meet and the ground, where the distance can be seen, is not shown. These are simple tricks which enable us to realise that time and space are devices invented by the human mind for its own convenience.

Now comes the other problem: substantiality or materiality. This is a boy, this is a girl, this is a tape-recorder, this is a room and these are walls—all these are denoted as such by the brain for our own conven-ience. The eyes perceive these objects as of a certain colour, as of a certain size, because the eyes are limited in their vision. As you know, human vision can only see a very small segment of the spectrum—our eyes are not equipped to see what a cat or dog can see. So when it comes to materiality, the external materiality is totally dependent upon the capacity of our brain and therefore of our senses.

When the brain comes to an end at the event known as death, questions like: where do I go?; how far do I go?; how long do I take to get there and what shape will I take later?—have absolutely no meaning. What is known as material space is a mere concept which arises in what is known as *chitta akasa*—the plane of the mind, the plane of thought. Does thought have a plane of its own? No. Thoughts, concepts, notions are floating in their billions and...don't complete that sentence.

We have already seen that as we wake up, 'I am' is the first thought that arises. Then, for some unknown reason, that 'I am' seems to be incomplete. Except in deep meditation, we can hardly ever confine our awareness to this mere 'I am'. 'I am' is always qualified by a name: 'I am So-and-so', or a functional attribute: 'I am waking up'. This 'I am' is what wakes up but immediately on waking, it associates itself and identifies itself with other thoughts and other functions. The reality of 'I am' is exactly the same as the reality of a girl or a boy, of space or time.

We ourselves don't exist; we ourselves don't belong to us yet we try to make other things belong to us! Silly! That is the fun. It is very much like dream where a person known as yourself arises and enters into a relationship with all sorts of other people. All the transactions then are very real. And, "In that world," says Vasistha, "there are beings as real as you are now."

When you conclude one dream you slip into another, often totally unrelated to the first. Even so there is really no birth and no death, these being parts of the same dream. In the next dream, just as in this dream, there are so many people, each one having his own mind and quite possibly dreaming his own dream. Therefore...worlds within worlds *ad infinitum*.

That we are all sitting here talking is a dream. But, because I decided at five o'clock in the morning (which is illusory, a stupid matter of convention) that I woke up, all the rest is supposed to be waking state, and what was before was sleep. This is how we have trained ourselves and we continue to religiously and faithfully continue the tradition. This is the *chitta akasa*: the plane of mind which seems to hang together because we have decided that it is so.

There is another colossal mystery, a colossal error which we regard as something very sacred. I have heard it said by the greatest thinkers and mystics that because we are scared, we want to belong to something, we want to identify ourselves with something—a religious group, a family group, a social group—and we want to feel that we are not standing alone. So as soon as the 'I am' thought arises it relates itself to a few others, enters into relationships and creates a 'we'— 'we brothers' or 'we religious people' or 'we students of Yoga'. That 'we' does not exist at all but it is the greatest mischief ever invented by man. All the other tragedies follow this 'we'-ing. Two total strangers suddenly become a 'we', each ready to fight and die for the other, calling it unselfishness, selflessness, patriotism and all sorts of crazy things.

The 'we' is the most dangerous thing in this world, created by the mind out of a false sense of security. It is interesting that recent American research in criminology has come up with the most obvious discovery that about eighty per cent of murders are committed by friends and relations! Why would a stranger come and attack me? He does not even know what I have or what I don't have; if I had a wife, she would know!

If I recognise that you are all strangers and if you recognise that I am a stranger in your midst, I think there will be more respect, there will be more care, there will be more caution, there will be more alertness and awareness. We don't know each other and we cannot know each other till we know ourselves.

In this dream called *chitta akasa* you create your own world. Vasistha seems to suggest that it is when you nod, when you wink, that a new creation arises. When you go to sleep at night the world is gone and when you wake up in the morning, you are creating a whole new world. When this happens to look like the one that was there before then it is accidental coincidence. If this morning's world looks like yesterday's world that is merely what you think it is. Whatever happens happens within you, right here.

Vasistha illustrates this with a rather interesting story of how this creation takes place. What on earth is this creation?

> There was a very pious couple who had ten sons. They were living an ideal life on a mountain top. Suddenly one day both the parents died. Such is life. The ten boys were completely shaken, shattered, shocked. They had a conference and one brother said: "My brothers, what shall we do? Our parents who lived such a marvellous life are lying dead now. This sort of life is not worth living. We should find a job that does not abruptly come to an end like this. What shall we become?"

Another brother said: "Let us become the emperor of the world."

"No, those fellows die. Let us become king of heaven."

"But after some time even the heavens are dissolved. Anything that comes to an end is fraught with misery, just as we are miserable now because our parents are dead."

Then one boy suggested: "Let us become creators of the universe."

As creator, as a god, you will live at least as long as your creation lives.

All the ten boys unanimously agreed to this, but the last one asked: "How do we become creators of the world?"

"Quite simple, meditation. Meditation will achieve everything."

Now, from here, please get into it.... Think that you are one of those ten boys.... Meditation can achieve everything in this universe. There is nothing that meditation cannot achieve.

"Brothers, close your eyes and contemplate: my head is the heaven; my feet are the earth; my skin is infinite space; my eyes are the sun and the moon; my breath is the air. Contemplate like this. Realise this."

Which means, wait until it becomes real!

They closed their eyes and determined that they would not open those eyes till this became the reality.

In the mean time (watch very, very carefully), no food, no drink, nothing...the bodies disintegrated. What happened to the contemplation that 'I am the universe'? That became the universe—ten different universes! It is as simple as that.

In that physical space there arose a firm notion or conviction that 'I am the creator of the world', and so it became. It is because of a deep-seated conviction that I am a man, that I am a human being, that I am an impotent, limited, finite little thing that I experience all these qualities in my own life. I am convicted by my own conviction and therefore I am imprisoned by my own experience.

There is a very funny catalogue of what is known as rebirth. I will give you just some fun. A man liked the scent of the lotus. One day while thinking of the scent of the lotus he died and because of that thought, he became a bee hovering around that lotus. The lotus closed at night trapping the bee inside. An elephant ate the lotus and the bee, finding itself being crushed inside the elephant, thought: "Oh, the elephant is killing me!" It died and became the elephant. Like this, there is a series.

Therefore, what we call rebirth is nothing but the crystallisation of our dominant dream. This goes on dream after dream till the *chitta akasa* is realised to be non-different from *chid akasa*. The external world exists only because I think I am the body, limited to the skin. There is division into external and internal only because I feel that I am the body and I am limited to the skin. When that skin is gone, what is internal and what is external? When that is realised we see that even when the body exists there is really no internal and no external. The body does nothing, it is just there. This seems to be the basic message of tremendous hope, of tremendous optimism, of inconceivable glory.

The Idea of I

We have seen that the mind is made restless by two factors: one, the movement of *prana* or life-force and two, the habit patterns—the *vasanas*, the conditioning, the psychological tendencies and predispositions. It is said that when these two come together the mind is activated. The mind becomes restless and the restlessness itself further strengthens the mental conditioning so that as this *prana* moves we get more and more confused and deluded. If you are ill or if you are made to fast for a few days you are not able to function brightly. This happens because the flow of *prana* is very weak.

Vasistha says: "Get hold of either one of these and the other also comes under your control." That is, if we are able to control the *prana* then the restlessness of the mind also comes under our control. By making the breath rhythmic, gentle, unhurried, unexcited, these qualities are reflected in the mind. If we are able to breathe gently the mind also functions in a gentle way. If the breathing is rhythmic the mind gains a certain order. If the breathing is unagitated the mind is also unagitated and still. This restlessness is not beyond our control. So you can obviously see that if this practice is taken to its fullness of complete suspension of *pranic* movement then the mental impressions are made inoperative. They will all be there but they have no energy to function. Just as, even when all the electrical equipment is there, if the main switch is off, the current is shut off with the result that the equipment becomes inoperative. That is when the mind is made 'no-mind'.

Taking the same analogy of electricity we can work from the other direction. The power is there but if we destroy all the equipment—the bulbs, the fans and so on—even if the main switch is on and the current can flow as much as it wants, none of these things will work. The current cannot flow because there is no channel. Therefore, control either of these (movement of *prana* or mental conditioning) and you will have control over both.

How does one abandon mental conditioning? Enquiry into its real nature and the discovery of this real nature is itself the abandonment of mental conditioning. Let us take an example from our normal life. I feel hungry and the first thought that arises in me is: "I am hungry." What does that mean? Certainly I am not hungry. There is hunger, a need for food, built into the physical organism. It is a biological conditioning that demands nourishment; so let the body have some food. On the same level, I look at the food and say: "I don't like this, I would like to have something else." Obviously that is not biological. Something else is operating here. If it is a simple biological urge the mouth will accept any food of a certain temperature (neither too low nor too high) which the body can digest as food—not stones and glass pieces. But the system does not demand chocolates! Now we are entering into something else: "I like this and I don't like that." Such a thing does not exist in a pure and simple biological system.

Enquiry, observation or contemplation eliminates the imaginary factors. What does that expression mean? The imaginary factor did not exist in the first place! So, what is eliminated? That is *maya*, that is our battle with illusion. An illusion cannot be eliminated. Unfortunately, we had assumed the non-existent to be real. That assumption is eliminated. When you walk outside at night, if something moves on the ground, you get frightened. You flash a light and find there is nothing. You wonder: "Why did that bear run away?" There was no bear, it was only the shadow of the branches cast in the moonlight. There was nothing there in the first place to run away from. That is the type of phenomenon that *vichara* or contemplation eliminates. That is the type of phenomenon that you abandon.

The truth cannot be abandoned. Biological functioning cannot be arrested at all and there is no need to arrest it; it has nothing whatsoever to do with you or me. The body is body—it is there, it will function and it will perish. The material world exists because someone (like the ten sons who became creators) was sitting in this area and contemplating: "I am the creator of the world; I am going to bring a lake into being and I am going to create earth, water, fire, etc." All this has come to be in his consciousness and we are all part of the dream-objects of that fellow. The whole earth is but a dream-object of some-one who is still dreaming. We have nothing whatsoever to do with it. It has not been created for us, it has not been created by us, it is not us. It can exist as long as it wants to exist, it can dissolve when it wants to dissolve, it has nothing to do with us.

Thus, contemplation or *vichara* leads to the complete elimination of imaginary factors and the realisation that there is nothing which is mine and that what I have been brought up to believe to be 'me' is not me. If all these are abandoned what exists is existence and that is 'me'. Even if 'I' exists it does not belong to me and therefore nothing that is related to this 'I', to the ego, is mine.

This realisation will arise only when the *chitta akasa* is seen not to be an entity in itself, not a self in itself, but one with the entire universe. Even those words are silly. Any other cosmetic treatment of the ego, of the *vasana* that produces and sustains this ego is blissful waste of time. To illustrate this Vasistha gives an extraordinarily beautiful story. In the text it is highly picturesque, highly romantic and exceptional. I will give you only the highlights:

> There was a royal couple: the king was known as Sikhidhvaja, the queen was known as Chudala. Both of them were interested in spiritual matters, so they studied. The queen was way ahead of the king in yogic attainments. She had found the key to enlightenment and had attained cosmic consciousness. As an added bonus she also had some psychic powers.

I have remarked again and again that what is known as enlighten-ment is very simple. Perhaps it is simpler than you and I imagine it to be. It is merely the getting rid of the ego-sense that does not exist in the first place! The problem is to enquire into its nature as a non-en-tity. That we are not prepared to do, and thereby hangs the tale.

> At one stage the king was filled with dispassion and he wanted to renounce everything and go away. The queen suggested some-thing very beautiful: "Everything has its own time and anything that is done out of time is not valued."

If you renounce the world when you are mature enough it becomes very fruitful, but not when the heart is still immature.

So the king continued to be a scholar. He had great knowledge of the scriptures but it was absolutely useless. One day he decided to leave the palace.

Early in the morning the queen awoke to find that the king's side of the bed was empty. (Although she had reached self-knowledge, the scripture takes care to note that even she was shocked.) Through her psychic powers she found out where he was. She knew what was going to happen, so she paid no more attention to it. She carried on the affairs of the state for nineteen years, paying an occasional visit to the king without his knowledge.

One day she decided the time was ripe to go and help him. But she thought if she went to him in her usual form he might run away from her, regarding her as *maya*. So she disguised herself as a radiant young boy called Kumbha and went to where the king was still practicing austerities. She hovered around in mid-air and looked at the king.

There is another interesting part here. As she was coursing in the air towards the king's hermitage, it seems there was excitement in her heart at meeting her husband and for a moment she wondered: "My God, I am an enlightened person to whom these relationships are illusory and yet the very thought that I am going to meet my husband excites me!" As long as one has the body these things are inevitable.

The king looked at the young radiant buddha and thought: "Lord, bless me. My wife says self-realisation is extremely simple; what it needs is real and total renunciation. I have renounced my kingdom, my palace and the royal pleasures. I have renounced my wife and family... what more do I have to renounce?"

Kumbha replied: "What is needed is total renunciation, not just partial renunciation. You must renounce not only the superficialities but the vital essence."

Sikhidhvaja looked at the hut—one matchstick and that was finished.

But the ascetic was not pleased. He said: "Why did you have to burn that down? If you did not like it, walk out: somebody else would occupy that place. Something useful has been destroyed. What is needed is real and total renunciation. The very essence of it."

The king said: "My God! He does not make it very clear." He

[130]

looked round. He had a water-pot and a stick—he threw them into the river.

The young man said: "If you did not want the water-pot you could have given it to some other ascetic. What is really needed is total renunciation of the essence. Shaving your head and such things are not of much use."

Everything is finished. Nothing except my body is left." The king was getting ready to destroy the body but the ascetic restrained him saying: "Who told you that this body is yours? There are worms in the earth, vultures and wild dogs waiting for it!"

Then the king asked: "What is mine?"

"Nothing... except the foolish idea that something belongs to you! That is the only thing to be renounced. The sense of ego towards the body and the sense of 'mine' towards what is related to the body are the two foolish ideas that you entertain and that should be forgotten. Merely realise that these are untrue."

The king said: "You are my guru now. Please, will you stay with me?"

Kumbha agreed. So the ascetic and the king became inseparable friends and continued to roam in the forest.

Then an idea arose in the queen. "I am staying with my husband. Why not enjoy life?"

Looking at the king, she felt attracted to him again. As long as there is the body, its natural functions will continue and only a fool will try to suppress them. Enlightenment has nothing to do with biological functions.

One day the queen disguised as the male ascetic, Kumbha, disappeared and came back in the evening, miserable and full of tears. The king asked: "I thought you were enlightened and enlightened people don't shed tears. What is wrong with you?"

She said: "There was an accident and I was cursed by a sage that every night I would be a woman. I am so miserable." He said: "What is wrong with that? During the daytime the body will be male and during the night it will be female." So the queen continued to live there, during daytime as a male companion and during the night as a female companion.

But still the queen's desire had not been fulfilled so one day she said to the king: "You are an enlightened man and I am also enlightened; there is absolutely nothing that we should or should not do. Every night I am going to be a woman and you are a man so why not let us get married?" So they got married again, in the forest.

But that is not the whole story. It is one thing to say: 'I don't regard anything as mine' and quite another thing to ensure that it is a realisation and not thought! We often confuse the two!

One day as the king was resting the queen, through her own magic powers, created a lovely pleasure garden and disappeared into it. The king woke up, found that the queen was missing, walked around and saw that she was in that pleasure garden enjoying intimacies with another young man. Quickly he excused himself and said: "I am sorry if I disturbed you; pardon me, please carry on and I will wait for you." Now Chudala decided that he really had the realisation that 'nothing is mine'. The whole scene disappeared and she told the king: "I just created this for fun to test you. You have come out victorious. There is no garden, there is no man except you."

As they were talking quietly, she also shed the form of Kumbha. The king suddenly looked at this person and said: "You know, you look very much like my wife." And then the queen said: "Yes, not only do I look very much like your wife, I am your wife! I thought you were foolish to abandon everything and come here, so I put on all these disguises in order to help you. Enlightenment is much easier than what you thought. It is merely an abandonment of 'I-ness' and 'mineness'." Then they returned to the kingdom and ruled for a long time.

The scripture comments: "Such should be all the wives in the world; such should be all the women in the world."

This is enlightenment. Thoughts are there, feelings are there, objects are there, but none of them is 'mine'. There is the realisation that the personality is but a bubble, a ripple that arises on the ocean, non-different from the ocean. The appearance can still continue as a ripple, it does not have to become flat, it does not have to abandon its form, but there is no conviction or feeling arising that this is 'I' or that this is 'mine'.

If there is a consciousness or awareness 'I am', that idea itself arises in the *chid akasa* or the plane of cosmic consciousness. Then there is no problem at all. But immediately it identifies itself with a few more entities floating around and creates a nucleus of what eventually becomes the *chitta akasa* or the mind, this mind takes on the impress of *vasanas*, memories and *samskaras*. From there on it becomes an individual—a personality migrating from one dream to another and enduring endless suffering. One has to live somewhere; one cannot abandon the world (that is an absurd expression—wherever you go there is a world). 'Abandoning the world' means abandoning the inner feeling that this is the world I live in, this is 'my' world and 'I' have a relationship with these objects or beings in this world. This is freedom of a very different quality, a beautiful freedom. He who is really and truly free in this sense is able to live a very full life without being trapped anywhere in it.

That was the purpose for which the teaching was given. After giving this message, Vasistha commands Rama: "Get up and engage yourself in the normal activities of the world, in appropriate action." When one observes the phenomenon called hunger, an appropriate action takes place and food is eaten. Then the craving for unhealthy food—chocolates and so on—drops away. If someone then offers you some chocolates you may consume them but without any craving. Thus, life continues and appropriate actions take place all the time without any dreadful craving, without any violent emotionalism and without the individual will coming into play at all. That is what is called 'living in tune with the Divine Will' and that is what my Guru called 'Divine Life'.

The Apparent Reality

We started off with an extremely simple discovery that unhappiness arises from pursuit of pleasure, pursuit of happiness. If we do not run after happiness we will never be unhappy: this is obvious. You can call it contentment, you can call it tranquillity, you can call it equilibrium—if there is no movement towards a thing called happiness there should be no unhappiness. You will be happy wherever you are, whatever you are doing.

So, why does one pursue pleasure or happiness at all? If you are observant you will see that it is because of a feeling that the happiness is out there in that object, and you must get it. At that point one's alertness is completely destroyed. This alertness is described variously in the different Yoga texts. Patanjali calls it *yama* and Vasistha calls it *satsanga, vichara*.

The Sanskrit word *yama* has many meanings. Two are important for us: one is self-restraint, discipline and the second is the name of the god presiding over death. I think there is a very significant connection. Self-discipline is not possible unless we are constantly conscious of death. If someone young and very closely related to you suddenly dies, in a moment of inner awakening, you say: "My God, one day I will die too. I must be very careful from now on because I may also die soon." This usually lasts until you get back home, then the same life goes on. Can that light, that shock, be sustained? It is not the final awakening or enlightenment because you have not really experienced death within yourself but you have a glimpse of the fact that you too will die.

I think you understand that discipline by others is not discipline at all. If you tell me I must do this and I do it, it is only superficial; inside I am rebellious. But self-discipline is also not possible unless this death is brought into daily life. It is then that the discipline takes on a wonderful new meaning. In English the word discipline also means study. I must study myself and then this discipline arises spontaneously.

One of the most important factors of *yama* is *satyam*. *Satyam* means truth, not only truthfulness, but truth. What is truth? Truth is not something which is crystallised, sitting there like a piece of stone, but truth is dynamic and therefore it is changing constantly. So there is a constancy in it and there is a change in it. That contains a paradox—'paradox' in the true sense of the word that this is something which cannot be taught by anyone. It cannot be taught but it can be caught if one is alert.

There is something constant and there is something constantly changing—when you see that you do not shy away from this thing called death. Nor do you disregard that which is for the moment. One gets a tremendous sense of balance which arises from this vision of truth. Then a disciplined life becomes natural. You are not going to run away from happiness because it floats down the stream of life. While it is there, enjoy it. When it goes, let it go. Change. Something else comes along which somebody else may call unhappiness but since it has come to me, it is most welcome. I do not ill-treat it and it does not ill-treat me. A little bit of unhappiness and it goes away. Thus the beautiful qualification of a student of Yoga, called equilibrium, becomes natural.

My guru, Swami Sivananda, used to say: "Remember God and remember death both together." Then you are established in the constant and you are able to participate in the changing. Then you are able to live your changing life but realise the eternal here and now. That is truth.

There are many problems arising from one's intelligence, one's mind, that constantly distract one's attention from truth. He who avoids all these distractions has brought death into his daily life. That which we have pushed away from our lives, imagining that by merely not thinking of it, it will go away, the yogi brings into his everyday life. This has a tremendous effect. When we remember death from moment to moment, realising that that is what is happening even to this body from moment to moment, then the past is cut off and we are not haunted by fear.

Does reality make us suffer or does the appearance make us suffer? Am I loving you or am I loving the appearance—the body with what appears to be a charming, beautiful face? This body is subject to change, so one must face this truth, this reality. It is when I love you as Mrs. So-and-so that I am unhappy when you go away. But if I love the truth—that which may dwell within that body which is more permanent, more constant—then as long as you are here in physical form (which is part of the total reality) I enjoy and appreciate it, and when you leave I am not unhappy at all. Balance again.

If I pursue happiness very soon I will realise that the only person that disturbs this happiness is myself, because I am running after a temporary thing called pleasure—I am mistaking the form for the spirit, the appearance for the reality. The reality does not make me suffer. Even the appearance does not make me suffer, but when I pursue that pleasure it makes me suffer. The understanding of that will enable me to drop all this pursuit of pleasure and there is instant unbroken happiness.

The lesson that was learned from the story of Chudala and Sikhidhvaja was that abandonment of the illusory idea of 'I am this' associated with the body and 'this is mine' associated with what is physical relationship is true renunciation and that brings to an end what is known as *ahamkara*.

Ahamkara is an 'I' (an ego) as distinct from 'you'; an ego as distinct from the rest of the universe. 'I am an independent being, totally independent from the rest of the universe'—as long as this idea or feeling or thought exists there is no end to the pursuit of pleasure, no end to the sorrow. But when the subject and the object collapse together at that time is revealed the most magnificent and absolutely simple truth that that which was between is the reality and always has been.

This is best illustrated with the example of the piece of paper given a short while ago. We will look into it briefly once more. I-you: 'I' being one end, 'you' being the other end. Having juggled this relationship into being, we endeavour to classify this relationship into 'you are my friend' or 'you are my enemy'; 'you are my rival', 'I like you', 'I don't like you', 'I love you', 'I hate you'. All these are born as secondary phenomena to the primary ignorant assumption of a duality. Such a duality does not exist in the paper. What is meant by 'I being one end, you being the other end'? What is the total paper in the context of our relationship? That alone is the reality. You assume that there are two ends and then hold one end up and the other down. This is top in relation to this bottom; this is bottom in relation to this top. Suddenly you discover that there is no top, there is no bottom, there is no end, there is no beginning; it is one piece of paper!

The object arises because the subject is there; 'you' exist because 'I' is there. Till this subject-object illusion collapses there is no end to sorrow. You can go to heaven if you want; you will get bored and then you will come back here. You can go to hell if you want—it may be a better place because you will be alert all the time, yet you will come back here. Anywhere, you are going to lead some kind of foolish dream life.

Nothing except *tattvajnana* or the direct understanding of the truth can put an end instantly to *vasana*. This is when you realise that there is nothing called 'my mind', there is nothing called 'me' and therefore whatever impressions there are in this universe, let them be, they are not 'mine'. That is *vasanakshaya*—annihilation of subtle desires or tendencies.

There are tendencies, yes, there are tendencies: a dog has a certain tendency, a cat has a certain tendency, a tree has a certain other tendency and the human body has a certain other tendency. But there is no 'me'. That is *manonasa*—destruction of the mind. There is no answer to the question "What is me?". There is no 'me' except memory, which remains memory. There is no *mano*—no mind—which says: "This is 'my' mind, this is 'my' memory, these are 'my' *vasanas*, these are 'my' habit patterns." The habit patterns may be related to the body or to the life—go ahead. But there is no 'me' to tyrannise this life-force which dwells in this body. It lasts as long as it lasts and it comes to an end when it wants to come to an end. Exactly like the trees, the dogs and cats and donkeys. *Vasanakshaya, manonasa, tattvajnana*—these three arise together.

When I stop blaming others for my unhappiness and when I see the truth that life itself brings happiness and unhappiness, pain and pleasure and so on, I am not offended or hurt by anyone in the world. If you call me an idiot, that is your problem, not mine. The yogi can never be hurt and that is a great blessing. When you are unhurt—and only then—do you become *ahimsa*, totally nonviolent. Nonviolence again is not something which you can do; all that you do is violent. But when you are completely unhurt then your relationship with everyone in this world is pure love.

This love arises spontaneously, from a discipline where you are constantly looking within. Then if someone calls you a wonderful person you look within to see if you are so wonderful. And if someone calls you an idiot again you look within to see if you are such an idiot. Therefore all are helping you and so you are friendly and in love with all life.

Towards the Goal

How do we go about freeing ourselves from this seemingly impossible trap—the tyranny of the mind, the tyranny of these psychological habit patterns? Physical habit patterns are not so oppressive as the psychological habit patterns. Vasistha does not suggest that there is a ladder or a step by step movement towards enlightenment because enlightenment is not the end product of a movement. Any movement is very likely to be movement away from the centre: movement away from the being into a dream world. However, as a concession to our inadequacy and ignorance, Vasistha suggests that it is more a study of the natural course or process of awakening rather than a stipulated method to be adopted. These are two very different things.

We often tend to commit this grievous error: we study the Yoga texts and then determine that we are going to be serious students of Yoga and serious students of Yoga must have truth, must be truthful, honest, loving... You cannot be 'must be loving'. Either you <u>are</u> loving or you are <u>not</u> loving. You cannot force yourself to love; you cannot force yourself to be honest; you cannot force your mind to be pure. And yet the yogis were not wrong. They studied serious students of Yoga and saw these qualities in them. So, one must discover how to bring about this purification of one's heart or mind.

The stages in the process that we are going to discuss now are thus stages seen in the process of awakening. You cannot listen to these words and apply them to your lives. It is imperative to see directly the problem of sorrow, the problem of the tyranny of the psychological tendencies and to realise the truth concerning the mind (if there is a mind).

Without understanding "the mind and its mysteries"—in the words of Swami Sivananda—without understanding the mind, its tricks and its mysteries, you cannot live. Life is an endless series and procession of sorrow. However, while trying to understand this mind, realise that the question "What is my mind?" cannot be answered by another. If the other person, even if he is a great psychologist, produces an answer, it is meaningless to you because it is his realisation not yours. And, at the same time, you cannot ask yourself "What is the mind?" for then the mind answers its own question. It is what I call psychological cannibalism: the mind produces its own offspring and chews them up. It is a waste of time!

So you cannot ask that question of others, you cannot find an answer in the mind itself, and without finding an answer, life is not worth living. When you confront this truth directly then what Vasistha calls *subheccha* arises. This is the first stage. *Subheccha* is a beautiful word but I am afraid it does not have such a beautiful translation in English. It is a holy desire—if one wants to translate it that way—a pious wish (though not the totally impotent pious wishes that you and I are familiar with). This is an auspicious wish, an auspicious desire, full of energy: "I <u>must</u> find an answer to this riddle. It is impossible to live with this tyrant called the mind; it is impossible to live in this dreadful state of ignorance." This is *subheccha*.

What form does this *subheccha* take? The resolve is to enquire into the nature of life, not the purpose of life. The yogi is not interested in the purpose of life because how does one know that there is a purpose? First of all there is the assumption that there is a purpose, which in turn asks the question "What is the purpose?" and then provides the answer "This is the purpose". That is not the truth at all. Instead of getting into all this unnecessary discussion, the yogi does not discourage people from assuming that there is a purpose of life but his question is: "What <u>is</u> life? What is this world? What is the truth concerning this? Who am I?" If the answer to this can be found the purpose manages itself.

Vicharana is the next stage or step which arises almost simultaneously with *subheccha*. It is not intellectual acrobatics. Swami Sivananda had no time or patience for intellectual acrobatics. Sorrow or unhappiness is not an intellectual affair, it is something that plagues our very life. It is real and therefore it must be solved. Not by merely defining it in terms of modern psychology or ancient Yoga philosophy or metaphysics but by facing and looking at it directly. That is called *vicharana*.

Vicharana is not *vichara*. Here there is an observation where the thought process is frozen. That is, you realise that you cannot wish unhappiness away. (If people could there would not be a single unhappy person in the world.) Sorrow cannot be wiped away by wishful thinking. And, sorrow cannot by wiped away by running away from it (running away aggravates sorrow) or by merely putting on some kind of nice cream. You can grin to your heart's content but the sorrow in your heart will reveal in your eyes. So you abandon the wish to abandon sorrow because you realise (a) you cannot do it and (b) you cannot live with this sorrow.

When this is very clearly understood, not intellectually but directly, there is an integral freezing of the mind. Incidentally, that is called *chitta vritti nirodhah* in terms of the Yoga Sutras of Patanjali. It is not suppressing the modifications of the mind but you are unable to find the answer to the question: "What is sorrow and how does it come to an end?" You do not give up and you cannot pick up; you cannot move, you cannot drop. Then you know what it is to be in a state of meditation. That is *vicharana*. *Vicharana* is not a thought process but a direct observation of the source of sorrow, of the nature of sorrow, of the very arising of sorrow.

If you have been following this for even these few minutes, you probably realise that the mind is becoming finer and finer—more and more transparent. Why is it so? If you have ever stepped into a muddy puddle you will understand this. The puddle seems to be very clear as you walk towards it but when you put your foot into it, immediately it becomes muddy. Step out of it, wait, and it settles down; it is clear again. Our restlessness to get rid of sorrow and to gain some happiness, some pleasure from somewhere, keeps the mind muddied, foggy. Allow it to settle down: it becomes transparent, subtle, clear.

That is the third stage, *tanumanasi*. There is a certain refinement and from being opaque the mind gradually becomes transparent. A glass pane is made opaque by a coating of silver on the other side so that you will only see your own reflection. To the person who is looking into a mirror, the whole world is 'myself', there is nothing more important than 'me', there is nothing more beautiful than 'me'.

Once the silver is wiped off the same glass becomes transparent and then you are able to see clearly what may be on the other side.

When the mind becomes fine, transparent, you are able to see the truth without being totally biased and self-centred. It is then that there is comprehension of purity. That is the next stage, *sattvapati*: the truth seems to be comprehensible, as it were. It is not, but it <u>seems</u> to be clear; it <u>seems</u> that you can grasp it. It looks as though you can see the very arising of sorrow. Can this be an illusion? Of course it can. Anything can be an illusion. But it looks as though you can see this. And it is possible that you see that the very attempt you are making to make yourself happy is itself the arising of sorrow. This is a strange thing. As long as there is dependency on an external object which you think contributes to your pleasure this whole game is not going to come to an end. This truth becomes clear at that point—*sattvapati*.

When this truth becomes clear, though not intellectually, there is *asamshakti*—the next stage. At that point there is...(it is difficult to translate)...psychological independence, or a certain state of inner freedom in which there is very clear understanding that happiness, unhappiness, pleasure, pain, may be real experiences, real feelings, but they are not dependent upon any object. The feeling that these arise from an object drops away. Those two words, 'drops away', are very important. It is not that you push the feeling away—there is no pushing away in Vasistha's Yoga. That which you push away takes you away. You cannot run away from your mind; it will follow you or you are following it all the time! *Asamshakti* is when all these ideas of dependency upon the object drop away because the truth is seen, because the mind is transparent. Pleasure: yes, there is pleasure, but that is experienced within; pain: yes, there is pain also, experienced within. These are not due to external causes. A couple more steps, then you realise there are no external causes at all!

The next stage is *padarthabhavana*. It is one of the most beautiful and intriguing expressions. The texts and the commentators' offerings treat it in two ways. We shall look at it in both ways, as both lead to the same point. This long word is broken into *padartha abhavana*—though etymologically they can mean two completely opposite things. *Padartha bhavana* means contemplating *padartha*; and *padartha abhavana* means the absence of *padartha*. I will explain what the word means. *Pada* means a word; *artha* means the meaning or the object denoted by this word; *bhavana* means contemplating it; *abhavana* means its absence. All these can apply to this stage in one's spiritual maturity or growth.

Padarthabhavana: there is a word but what is its meaning, where is its meaning? There is no meaning in words whatsoever except the meaning you assume that these words have. This, I believe, was Ramana Maharshi's favourite theme. Nothing in this universe sits on your shoulder and quietly whispers into your ears: "You know, I am a chocolate, an ice cream, a house'! That is; but that becomes chocolate, ice cream, house, in your mind. The word exists; the world exists (the difference between them is just one 'l'), but it is some inner mischief-maker that links these two and then, desires, hates, and so on.

Can you, in a similar vein, examine the meaning of each word and discover for yourself whether the thing that you think the word denotes is real or assumed? A man looks at his wife and says: "Honey." Wait a moment!...Do you need any more explanation? When one engages oneself in this seriously then one begins to play with words. And words have no meaning whatsoever except the meaning that your own brain imputes to them, attributes to them, superimposes upon them.

Then suddenly the other meaning of the word *padarthabhavana* becomes clear. The words are there, the sounds are there but they do not have a corresponding object—*padartha abhavana*. Maybe it is a digression but let us remind ourselves here that this does not mean that sugar will not taste sweet to an enlightened person. The life-force that lives in the body will react appropriately to all situations. The living being knows how to live in all situations, acting appropriately in each situation. Vasistha even says: "You can cry if you want. You can laugh if you want—bearing in mind the social customs and so on—but in your own heart you are not fooled." Something is called pleasure, it is not pleasure. Something else is called pain. Except to the extent that it is called pain and the mind and the brain have been trained to experience this as pain, there is no pain. There is no pain, there is no pleasure—*padarthabhavana*. Then the objects disappear.

At that point one realises that the world which, in ignorance, is considered to be outside of oneself is really not outside of oneself. It is like a mirror image. The entire universe is reflected in 'me'. And the 'me' being just a mirror, there is nothing there. 'I' am not an entity but a mirror. And we are all being reflected *ad infinitum* in the dual mirrors placed facing each other. The pleasure that seems to come from your company is experienced within and so is essentially independent of the object. And it is the subject (that arises along with this experience) that characterises this experience as pleasure. It is not as simple as that.

Can one free oneself from all this? It can be done by abandoning the idea of self and at the same time allowing the idea of an object independent of oneself also to drop away. These are merely words which have no meanings at all in the sense that they have corresponding objects. These words are understood to mean something only within you. It is the brain that attributes meanings to these words, otherwise there is no world as such.

When this truth is clearly seen there is transcendence of all; a state which is nominally described as *turiya*. The sage at that stage transcends all objective experience even though he may continue to exist in this world and to experience pleasure and pain, happiness and unhappiness in the eyes of others.

A very beautiful verse occurs in the Yoga Vasistha which is often quoted by Ramana Maharshi: "His life is like the movement of your feet towards a destination you have decided upon." That is, if you decide to walk to a certain place, your feet walk there. Even though walking itself means a million little adjustments from moment to moment, you are almost unaware of them. Once the decision is made your feet take you there. In the case of an enlightened person, enlightenment has been the goal and life flows on in an enlightened way, or as God wills it. That is a life that is divine life, that is free from sorrow. Such is the glorious message that is placed before us by Vasistha in the Yoga Vasistha and that our guru, Swami Sivananda, exemplified and illustrated in his daily life.

Consciousness Is

A study of the Yoga Vasistha destroys all your values. It makes life look ludicrous—which it is. Once the entire value structure is smashed there is nothing worth aspiring for! You don't want to run after anything. If it comes, it comes; if it doesn't come, that is also good. First desire and craving drop away. Nothing is worth craving for—not because craving is something which is going to lead you to hell (hell or heaven are not important either)—but the whole thing is made unimportant, valueless. Why will you crave for something which is valueless? That is perhaps what Jesus meant when he said: "Unless you are like little children you cannot enter the kingdom of heaven." A baby has absolutely no special value for anything. It picks up the microphone, licks it, turns away and picks up something else, plays with it—it's gone. It is not attracted to anything by value.

Are you not attracted to <u>something</u>? Yes, naturally, you are attracted to something in strict accordance with nature and nothing more. When you are hungry you are attracted to food. When you are tired you are attracted to bed. When it is very cold you lie under the blanket. These are determined by nature. When you are of the proper age and some children are to be born you are attracted to each other. Don't call this love.

That is the simple lesson that emerges from the Yoga Vasistha. When everything has been devalued, the one valueless (in the sense of beyond all valuation) feature remains, and that is consciousness. That consciousness is steady because it is undeflected by craving, desire or pursuit of pleasure. It is not veiled by hate, by vanity, by ego-sense, by self. It stands as clear as daylight, for ever and ever and ever.

What is called the memory (or the 'me' or the ego) has this awareness as its core. Consciousness is the very substance of memory, of all concepts. There is no concept, whether you call it craving, desire, hate or selfishness—whatever be the labels you stick upon it. You peel that label off and see that the stuff is consciousness. Consciousness is—all else appears to be.

Then just one more lesson becomes abundantly clear. If this lesson is not clearly grasped we can be led astray, even by the study of the Yoga Vasistha. When you are undeflected by pursuit of pleasure, hate or selfishness and the mind is calm even the *chitta akasa* is calm and the *chid akasa* is brilliant. Life flows with all its ups and downs. Sometimes you are miserable and then you begin to wonder why you are miserable. It is not important—what is wrong with being unhappy sometimes? So you are not trying to get rid of it, you are merely looking at it: "What is this new phenomenon?" Suddenly you realise that that unhappiness is directly related to a craving that arose. There was a craving and that craving couldn't be fulfilled, therefore there was this frustration. Without thinking 'I am miserable', you see the unhappiness or frustration related to the craving—not to 'me', because the 'me' does not exist. There was a craving (a hope). It arose—you don't know why—and when it was not fulfilled there was frustration, unhappiness.

A clear awareness of the simple truth that where there is pursuit of pleasure there is bound to be frustration prevents the hope from being linked to the self. That is all. I am not saying you will go to hell if you pursue pleasure—there is no such value in the pleasure or in its avoidance—but this is seen as cause-and-effect at their own level, not at the level of the infinite consciousness. If you pick up a piece of cloth and drop it in the swimming pool it becomes wet. This is a pure and simple cause-and-effect phenomenon which you can observe.

At the mental and psychological level, the *chitta akasa* level, this cause-and-effect phenomenon applies too. That is, where there is pursuit of pleasure there is a possibility of frustration.

Let this truth 'Where there is hope, fear is possible' soak into you. Don't do anything more, nothing more is necessary. That awareness itself will take care of life's ups and downs and keep the *chitta akasa* (or the mind) tremendously alert, so that even by mistake it does not bestow a positive value upon anything in this world. Then you are instantly freed from what we call the self, from birth and death and therefore from any unhappiness in life.

Epilogue:
The Key to
God-Consciousness

Guru Purnima day is considered a special day to honour the guru. There are a number of legends associated with this day. They say the great sage, Vyasa, commenced composing a great text on this day. There is also a tradition among the wandering monks of India that from about this time, for four months, they do not wander, for the simple reason that this is the monsoon season. It is a mark of the wise man that he turns the best part of a disadvantage into an advantage. The wandering life has to be abandoned because it is very uncomfortable to walk in the rain day in and day out. So these monks, swamis, stay in one place and during these four months they hold *satsangs* and daily discourses on various topics. In this way the disadvantage of the monsoon season is turned into a spiritual advantage. Nowadays we do not wander on foot anymore and so the external season, the external climate, does not affect us very much. But there is an inner climate.

What is the inner climate of the Guru Purnima? We celebrate the guru, we remember the guru and some of us rededicate ourselves to the guru on this auspicious day. A great saint called Kabir asked: "If God and guru are both standing in front of me who should I greet first?" As soon as the question arose in his heart the answer was also found. I bow to the guru because it is the guru who showed me who God is. If you repeat this sentence a few times a new light arises in your heart. It is the guru that shows me who God is. Conversely, one who shows you God is guru.

There is a bold and beautiful declaration in the Yoga Vasistha:

"He is a guru who is able to give rise to God-consciousness in the disciple by a look, by a touch, by a verbal communication or by grace."

It is because this person is able to do that to the disciple that the guru becomes a guru. Otherwise there is no guru. The guru does not appoint himself, nor does the disciple appoint the guru. When this mighty event takes place, when you are inwardly awakened and when you become God-conscious, he through whose grace this happened to you, whatever be the manner by which that grace was transmitted, is the guru. And, if it has not happened, the guru has not happened.

The guru is the light dispelling the darkness of doubt, confusion and spiritual ignorance. It is not a sin to be unenlightened as long as you are on the spiritual path and looking for the light. The guru will come and when that guru appears you cannot make a mistake because he reveals the truth, God or reality in your own heart. In a manner of speaking this inner revelation is the guru. Since this person, or whatever it may be, was responsible, directly or indirectly, for this tremendous spiritual event, you ascribe the status of guru to the personality because that is the link between 'me' and the Divine. If that veneration has not taken place the guru has not been found.

One needs a guru and the guru becomes valid and meaningful when confirmation is needed or when in a state of despair. Otherwise the guru is just another piece of furniture. A guru is only meaningful when you have reached that point of total despair where you have seen the vanity and futility of life and, perhaps, within yourself you have struggled hard to resolve the problems that present themselves to you through an observation of life. Then, completely bewildered and puzzled, you are unable to move one inch. You are not prepared to go back because you have seen that it is all rubbish, but you do not know which way to go. It is then that a guru becomes beautiful and meaningful.

It is an immature mind that appoints, disappoints and dismisses gurus. There is a book called Hunting for a Guru in India. The gurus are not animals to be hunted, so, naturally, when people hunt, the gurus run away! The gurus are not some kind of employees whom you appoint, disappoint and dismiss. Guru is something that happens and when it happens it is utterly unmistakable and even when it is about to happen, standing in front of that person, you realise: "This is he!'

A military officer once asked me: "Is it possible that this afternoon you bumped into an incarnation of God and failed to recognise it, him, her? How do you recognise an incarnation of God?" What is the answer? The scriptures specifically say that the great incarnations, Rama, Krishna, Buddha, Jesus, appeared to be human, behaved like human beings. Even so the great masters are human. We might bump into one of them in a supermarket tomorrow morning. How do we recognise one? I have no answer.

In reply to the colonel's question, I asked: "How do you find one specific cow among a hundred when all the cows look alike? There is only one way to do that: take the calf into the herd and let it go. It goes straight to the mother." How does the calf recognise its mother? There is no explanation. In a similar way you will recognise your guru and in a similar way you will also recognise when you bump into an incarnation of God.

It is not by external marks or external behaviour that one distinguishes the holy from the unholy. Krishna specifically commands that the wise man should behave like the unwise man, though inwardly there is a big difference—one is attached, the other is unattached; one is greedy, the other is not greedy. There is a mysterious something in that holy person so that when you stand in front of him you know: he is the guru.

Gurudev has also mentioned in one of the writings: "He in whose presence you are elevated, in whose presence your doubts are at rest, in whose presence you enjoy peace and bliss at heart, he is the guru." Another young disciple of Baba Muktananda gave a brilliant talk when he said: "You might come across a great saint, a great yogi whom the entire humanity minus one, adores as guru. But if you are that one, he is not your guru. The fact that everybody else is inspired by this person is of no value to you whatsoever. Leave him alone and try to find your guru."

How does one find one's guru? What does the guru do to the disciple? The Yoga Vasistha is a dialogue between Rama and Vasistha. One day as Rama was listening to Vasistha he went into an elevated state and everyone in the audience recognised that something had happened to this student. The great sage who initiated the whole drama turned to Vasistha, the teacher, and said: "Vasistha, you are the

son of the Creator, you are a great sage, but now, by putting Rama into this exalted state through *shaktipata*, you have proved that you are his guru." The function of the guru is the transmitting of something called *shakti*. This can happen by a mere look, a touch, a thought or by word of mouth. In the case of Rama and Vasistha perhaps all four
were involved.

Shaktipata is an extremely simple yet profound expression which literally means dropping *shakti*. What is that *shakti*? It is of the power of enlightenment. The guru is an enlightened person and his power is poured into the disciple. Is this possible? The famous Kabir says: "Why do you doubt that such a thing can take place? A man suffering from tuberculosis sits at a very respectable distance in front of you and merely coughs and you go home with the disease! If a minute virus or microbe can have such power what about enlightenment or God-consciousness? Do you mean to say that God-consciousness is less power-ful than a virus? Even so," says Kabir, "if you sit in front of an enlightened person and he merely looks at you, you get the same infection." This God-consciousness is highly contagious.

Does *shaktipata* entirely depend upon the master's grace? And, will *shaktipata* transform everybody? If so, why did it not happen on a mass scale when Krishna, Rama, Jesus or Buddha were here? It is inevitable that when you approach a God-conscious person you must catch the contagion of God-consciousness. But how soon the conta-gion will take effect depends upon your qualification. *Shaktipata* will never go in vain. If you are too dumb, dull and dense now that seed sown in your heart will germinate in perhaps fifty thousand years time!

There seems to be a decidedly strong suggestion that whereas the guru's awakening grace is there, it will become effective only to the extent that you are a true disciple. Gurudev Swami Sivananda once told someone: "It is easy to find a guru, it is very difficult to find a disciple." A disciple is a very rare phenomenon.

What is the cause of enlightenment? When the disciple's heart has become perfectly pure then God-consciousness arises in that heart. But then, is the guru so important? Yes, very important. Vasistha uses a double negative to state: "Guru does not produce God-conscious-ness in you, but God-consciousness does not arise in you without a guru." The guru is not the cause of the disciple's enlightenment but God-consciousness is not attained without the help of a guru. Vasistha also gives a story:

A very wealthy, miserly man was walking through a pine forest. He had a copper coin in his hand and the coin dropped. Frantically, he began to search for it. As he dug deeper and deeper into the pine bed he suddenly found a precious gem, the philosopher's stone, which is capable of turning all metal into pure gold, and he took it home. Now the question is asked: How did this man come by the philosopher's stone? Was it because he was looking for the copper piece? If he was looking for the copper piece he should have found that copper piece. But while he was engaged in searching for that copper piece he came by this precious gem. If he had not been looking for that copper piece he would not have found this gem.

Do all people who look for a copper piece find a precious gem? No. It is not as though the guru waves a magic wand and you attain God-consciousness but without a guru you do not attain God-consciousness.

What is important is that the heart should become pure. Therefore, the spirit of discipleship is extremely important. If you have devotion to the guru and a heart to heart contact then in that presence there is a verbal and a non-verbal dialogue. In that dialogue the cloud is dispersed. Therefore, another qualification for a real student of Yoga is a complete and total devotion to the guru. Then enlightenment, in the words of Vasistha, is easier than crushing a flower that lies in your hand. Even to crush a flower that lies in your hand needs some effort, but for enlightenment no effort is necessary.

If we can, day in and day out, strive to be better disciples then the guru will be there. Wherever a true disciple is, there is the guru. That true discipleship itself is the guru and hence, in a characteristic way, Gurudev emphasised at every turn that the guru is very necessary. Simultaneously he turned the other way and said: "Don't be a guru, don't think you are a guru." In that lies the truth. Be a disciple; then you will see the whole universe as your guru.

We start with a personalised form of the guru, but this experience of the presence of the guru expands and envelops the whole universe. That is what I saw in Gurudev Sivananda. He himself treated everybody as his guru or as his teacher from whom he learned something. That the great and mighty guru felt that he was everyone's disciple was a fantastic lesson we learned at his feet. He used to call himself an eternal student. In such a spirit of discipleship dwells the highest wisdom, the key to God-consciousness.

Afterword

Swami Venkatesanandaji Maharaj was a tireless traveller and persuasive preacher. He had a rare combination of wonderful talents—deep scholarship, ability to chant thousands of passages with traditional accents, knowledge of various types of worship, proficiency in Yoga, an endless stock of devotional songs which he could sing in his melodious voice and which he could teach others to sing in chorus, the power to get absorbed in meditation and, above all, a sweet and genial personality. It is no wonder that hundreds of earnest seekers flocked to him wherever he went. In the midst of his crowded programmes he found time to write a number of useful books and set up a book trust. As a photographer he was superb!

Swami Venkatesanandaji established an ashrama in a very beautiful part of Rose Hill, in Mauritius. A group photo was once taken after one of his many meetings there. Myself and Swami Kritanandaji—my successor in the Ramakrishna Mission, Vacoes, Mauritius—stood on either side of him along with his devotees. That photo is a welcome reminder to me of many other occasions when we were together in different parts of South Africa. Swami Venkatesanandaji's contact has transformed many lives and created groups of dedicated workers everywhere. Some have gladly taken vows of celibacy and become torchbearers offering their inborn talents for the service of God <u>in</u> man, or <u>as</u> man.

The Mahabharata, composed by Sage Vyasa, has a hundred thousand verses. It is the longest poem in the world. The next longest is Sage Valmiki's Yoga Vasistha. It has thirty-two thousand verses. The third longest is the well known Ramayana of Sage Valmiki. It has twenty-four thousand verses. The story of Sri Rama and Sita as narrated by the great sage—contemporary of Sri Rama and his two sons, as shown in the poem itself—has formed the basis for many compositions which differ from it and from one another in some details. But the main turns of the story are the same in all versions. They all describe the scene where Queen Kaikeyi spoke on behalf of the 'tongue-tied' Dasaratha and brought about Rama's exile and the installation of her own son, Bharata, as heir apparent. According to Valmiki, Rama's responce was polite and unforgettable. Said he to Kaikeyi: "Commanded by you, I would myself gladly, in favour of Bharata, part with not only the kingdom and my (private) property but even Sita and my beloved life itself. How much more joyfully shall I part with these when enjoined by my father, the Emperor himself, and that too, with intent to please you and to honour the boons he gave you?"[1] And again: "O Revered One, I do not desire to live in the world as a slave to material gains. Know me to be devoted to immaculate righteousness like the Rishis... Surely you do not recognise any good point in me since you had to speak to my father (about such a trivial thing) though you had greater authority over me (than my father)."[2]

This spirited, slightly reproachful, but subdued response reveals two aspects of Sri Rama's character. One is his divinely benign attitude and the second, what he gained from the instructions of his family preceptor, Vasistha. It is these very instructions that form the subject matter of Yoga Vasistha. It was only after the teachings were completed that Sage Visvamitra took Rama and Lakshmana from the palace, taught them the use of different weapons and made them capable of defending the hermitages from the attacks of miscreants. Swami Venkatesanandaji deals with some of the main principles along with the stories taught by Sage Vasistha. One interesting story is that of King Sikhidhvaja and his wonderful Queen, Chudala. Taught by Chudala in the guise of Kumbha, the king found it immaterial whether he lived in the forest or went back to rule the kingdom—since illumination takes consciousness to a totally transcendental level. What we call our 'waking state' becomes, to the illumined Soul, the field for a blissful game beyond the range of words and concepts. One abiding in such a state is called 'Liberated-in-life'.

Years ago Dr B.L. Atreya published a book, Yoga Vasistha and Modern Thought. In it he has shown, in different chapters, the essence of Vasistha's teachings and quoted side by side parallel passages from the writings of numerous modern thinkers. We present below a few extracts from Dr. Atreya's book.

The mind is the creator of the world; whatever it wills, in whatsoever way, that takes place.[3]

One attains whatever one strives for with a desire. No one else is responsible for one's achievements.[4]

Mind is the creator and enjoyer of all happiness and misery and of all impulses. In fact, man is nothing but what the mind makes him.[5]

The body is a form that has been assumed by the mind through intense desire and that has been made visible by repeated attempts.[6]

Mental worries give rise to bodily diseases. The latter are cured when the former are cured.[7]

When the mind is perfected the entire world of the individual becomes perfected and is filled with nectar.[8]

To match such truths indicated by Sage Vasistha, Dr. Atreya quotes from many modern writers. Here are a few examples:

Thought is the stuff of which things are made. Mind is all. It is everything. All matter is but a materialisation of consciousness. Control thought and you control destiny.[9]

The limit of your thought will be the limit of your possibilities.[10]

Your own thoughts, desires and aspirations comprise your world and to you all that there is in the universe of beauty and joy and bliss or of ugliness and sorrow and pain is contained within yourself. By your own thoughts you make or mar your life, your world, your universe. As you build within by the power of thought, so will your outward life and circumstances shape themselves accordingly. When the heart is pure all outward things are pure.[11]

From Chapter 42, "The Liberated Life":

The liberated living man is free from attachment and lives like an emperor.[12]

Such people are not disgusted with the people of the world, nor are the latter disgusted with them.[13]

They discriminate between acts and come to decisions quickly.[14]

They understand others' minds, behave gently and speak sweetly and softly.[15]

As a lion comes out of the cage, he who is liberated in life gets free from the shackles of caste, religion, stage of life, traditional morality and scripture and goes out of the nest of the world.[16]

He is a youth among the young, aged among the aged, brave among the brave, a child among children and sympathetically miserable among the miserable.[17]

He engages himself in all his duties without any personal desire but with a feeling that the Cosmic Will is being done through him.[18]

His face does not become unusually bright in prosperity nor does it become dull in misery. He stays equal-minded in all states.[19]

The home of such householders whose minds are well balanced and who have cast away the evils of egotism are as good as solitary abodes in the forest.[20]

As in the spring season the beauty and grandeur of trees increase, so the power, intellect and lustre of one who has realised the truth increases evermore.[21]

To match these ideas of Sage Vasistha, Dr. Atreya quotes from many modern writers:

Feeling the unity of himself and the universe, the man who lives in spirit is no more a self-centred individual, but a vehicle of Universal Spirit...He is able to face crisis in life with a mind full of serenity and joy... These rare and precious souls, filled with the spirit of the whole, may be said to be world-conscious. They have the vision of the self in all existence and of all existence in the self...They have an abiding realisation of the secret oneness which is the basis of universal love...the life of the seer takes on a new depth, a marked increase in coherence and character. There is a general enrichment of personality. It is more of life and not less.[22]

There is no bondage in Heavenly Life. There is Perfect Freedom...Heavenly Freedom is freedom from passion, from opinions, from the tyranny of the flesh and the tyranny of the intellect—this first, and then all outward freedom, as effect to cause...Greatness is never obtrusive. It works in silence seeking no recognition.[23]

(The illumined person) can enjoy solitude but he does not fear the society of man: he is a child with children, joyous with the young, staid with the aged, patient with fools, happy with the wise. He smiles with all who smile, he mourns with all who weep. He takes his part in all festivities, sympathises in all mournings, applauds all strength of mind, is indulgent to all weaknesses: never offending anyone, he has never to pardon, for he never thinks himself offended.[24]

Accepting from the human standpoint the value of spiritual instruction for all, we can see how the teachings of Sage Vasistha were fully reflected in the behaviour of Sri Rama, in his reactions to the baffling and painful situations that confronted him. He manifested the highest magnanimity, serenity, truthfulness and selflessness in all his thoughts and actions. He has set an example for all of us to copy.

Swami Venkatesanandaji has placed us all under a deep debt of gratitude by taking this wonderful book, Yoga Vasistha, and bringing out some of its valuable teachings. Thanks are due to Swami Venkataramani for editing and publishing this volume for the benefit of all sincere spiritual aspirants.

SWAMI NISREYASANANDA

Ramakrishna Vedanta Society
35, Rhodes Avenue, Belvedere
Harare, Zimbabwe

1st June 1986

NOTES

1. Valmiki's Ramayana, Book II, Canto 19, verses 7 & 9.
2. Ibid., verses 20 & 24.
3. Yoga Vasistha, VIb, 139:1
4. Ibid., IV, 13:11
5. Ibid., III, 116:24
6. Ibid., VIa, 28:34
7. Ibid., VIa, 81:38
8. Ibid., V, 21:34
9. Charles Gilbert Davis, The Philosophy of Life
10. Orison Swett Marden, How to Get What You Want
11. James Allen, Book of Meditation
12. Yoga Vasistha, V, 93-24
13. Ibid., VIb, 98:2
14. Ibid., VIb, 98:4
15. Ibid., VIb, 98:3
16. Ibid., VIb, 192:9
17. Ibid., V, 17:14

18. Ibid., V, 6:1
19. Ibid., III, 9:6
20. Ibid., V, 56:22
21. Ibid., V, 76:20
22. Dr. Radhakrishnan, An Idealist View of Life
23. James Allen, The Heavenly Life
24. Eliphas Levi, The Paradoxes of the Highest Science